THE MENU

EVE MARLEAU

'This unexpected, quirky and always revealing romp back in time, establishes the menu as a fantastic source for anyone interested in food, cookery or social history'
HESTON BLUMENTHAL

'Eve Marleau's knowledgeable tour of the tables of grand diners, families and workers across the globe eloquently describes how and why our menus have changed over the last two centuries; from turtle to instant noodles; the Suffragettes' lentil cutlets to Duke Ellington's hotdogs. Studying the menu is a brilliant way to show who and what decides how those dishes get onto the table; the passion, hard work and innovation in kitchen, canteen or laboratory; our snobbishness and generosity; big business, politics, war and want. Above all, every delicious menu is a reminder of our shared appetite for good food and rewarding company.'
PEN VOGLER, EDITOR OF PENGUIN'S GREAT FOOD SERIES

THE MENU

MEMORABLE MEALS
FROM ESCOFFIER AT THE
RITZ TO A SUFFRAGETTES'
VICTORY DINNER TO THE
FIRST MEAL ON THE MOON

EVE MARLEAU

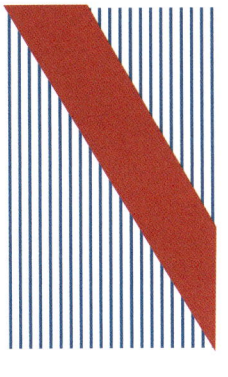

Foreword by
POLLY RUSSELL

BRITISH LIBRARY

First published 2019 by
The British Library
96 Euston Road
London NW1 2DB

Text copyright © Eve Marleau 2019
Images copyright © The British Library Board and other named copyright holders 2019

British Library Cataloguing in Publication Data
A catalogue record for this publication is available from the British Library

ISBN 978 0 7123 5300 7

Designed by Will Webb Design

Printed and bound in Italy by Printer Trento

All illustrations from the Collections of the British Library except:

19-20 Smithsonian Library.; 22 Royal Pavilion & Museums, Brighton & Hove; 34 The Women's Library collection, LSE Library; 36 Peter Stackpole/The LIFE Picture Collection/Getty Images; 42 Gregory Varnum/Wikicommons. Creative Commons Attribution Share-Alike 4.0 International License; 44 Stefano Politi Markovina/Alamy Stock Photo; 46 New York Public Library; 50-51 Library of Congress; 52 Photo Carol M. Highsmith, Library of Congress; 54 Granger Historical Picture Archive/Alamy Stock Photo; 62, 64-65, 66, 68, 70 New York Public Library; 72 Cyril Critchlow Collection, Blackpool Central Library; 76 © John Lawrence; 78 Courtesy of the Fat Duck; 84, 86-87 Royal Collection Trust/© Her Majesty Queen Elizabeth II 2014; 88 Photo 12/Universal Images Group via Getty Images; 90 The Women's Library collection, LSE Library; 96 Library of Congress; 102 Courtesy Taj Hotel Group; 108, 110-111 John F. Kennedy Presidential Library; 112 Alison Shelley/Getty Images; 116, 118-119 Library of Congress; 120 New York Public Library; 122 Charles Hewitt/Picture Post/Getty Images; 126 NASA; 140 National Library of Australia; 182 Michael Ochs/Getty Images; 194 Museo Picasso, Barcelona, Spain/ Index Fototeca/Bridgeman Images. © Succession Picasso/DACS 2019; 196 Fitzwilliam Museum; 198 NARA; 200 Photo William Gottlieb, Library of Congress; 206 Shawshots/Alamy Stock Photo; 210 Granger Historical Picture Archive/Alamy Stock Photo; 214 Vittoriano Rastelli/Getty Images; 216 NARA; 218 Jacques Lange/Paris Match via Getty Images; 220 Robert Marquardt/Getty Images.

CONTENTS

FOREWORD   6

INTRODUCTION   8

STARTERS   **14**
- Menu Firsts   16
- Food Inventions   42
- Iconic Menus   62

MAINS   **80**
- Meals That Made History   82
- Social Changes That Made Menus   114
- The History of Cookbooks   130

DESSERTS   **160**
- Famous Feasts   162
- Food in the Arts   184
- Last Meals   206

FOREWORD

THERE IS SOMETHING INHERENTLY tantalising about a menu – it's simultaneously a promise, an invitation and a set of directions. In French, the word for menu, 'carte', also means map – and no wonder. While recipes tell you how to cook, menus suggest what you should eat and in what order. They plot your journey through a meal and as such, they direct and tempt in equal measure.

Menus, or bills of fare, appear in cookery books and manuscripts from the medieval period, but we have the French to thank for menus in the form that we know them today. Although taverns and inns provided shelter and food for weary travellers from the Middle Ages onwards, 'restaurants', where patrons sat at their own tables and selected from a choice of dishes available on a menu, originated in Paris in the mid-eighteenth century. Restaurant menus appeared in various forms – scrawled on a chalkboard, read aloud by a waiter or written on paper and handed to the patron. At the start of the nineteenth century, menus tended to be written or printed on a large, single page with small, closely packed type. By the middle of the century, as restaurants proliferated and competed for wealthy customers, menus were often placed in leather-covered booklets complete with silken cords.

Compared with other historical evidence – letters, newspapers, official records and diaries, for instance – menus have received relatively little attention. Partly this is because they are generally ephemeral – written to reflect the menu of the day or the week and discarded once they are out of date. Recently, however, historians, archives and libraries have started to make concerted efforts to collect and curate menu collections. Menus are increasingly recognised as rich, complex sources. They tell us about availability and price, technological innovation, aspiration and expectation, fads and fashions and long-held traditions.

From the distance of decades or centuries, menus transport us back to many different pasts. In this deliciously eclectic collection, we can journey to the Imperial Palace for the coronation of the last Tsar of Russia, or revisit childhood with a menu for school dinners. Menus allow us to visualise meals enjoyed, to picture long-lost interiors and to eavesdrop on imagined conversations. As such, menus are curiously compelling. Some menus provide a voyeuristic opportunity to join a private party. Take, for instance, Elvis and Priscilla Presley's wedding breakfast menu of

Champagne, oysters and, with a concession to personal taste and not convention, southern fried chicken. Other menus are inextricably bound up with the public politics of a particular moment. When the suffragettes sat down to eat a four-course menu at the Minerva Café in London in 1918, the choice of a vegetarian restaurant was as radical at the time as seeking the vote. This book, bringing together such a wide selection of different menus, is a veritable feast for anyone interested in social history, food history and the evolution of dining out.

POLLY RUSSELL

LAND OF THE SKY.

Southern Railway Company
BIDS YOU WELCOME
COMPLIMENTARY DINING CAR SERVICE
ON OCCASION OF THE FORTY-SIXTH ANNUAL
MEETING OF THE AMERICAN ASSOCIATION OF GENERAL
PASSENGER AND TICKET AGENTS

ASHEVILLE, N. C., OCTOBER 15TH-17TH, 1901

FRUIT

MALT BREAKFAST FOOD

Apple Sauce   Preserves

Rolls

Coffee   Chocolate   Tea

BROILED POMPANO   STEWED OYSTERS

Raw Tomatoes

CHOPS   SIRLOIN STEAK   HAM

RAIL BIRDS ON TOAST
Fried Samp

BAKED POTATOES   FRIED SWEET POTATOES

EGGS AND OMELETS

SAUSAGE AND RICE CAKES

BREAKFAST

     En route, October 18, 1901.

INTRODUCTION

A MENU IS, IN ESSENCE, A LIST: it fuels anticipation, expresses creativity, and ultimately, is a vehicle of choice. When considered in this light, it could be said that these 'lists' – read in millions of places, millions of times a day, in millions of different circumstances – are some of the most useful tools when it comes to the exploration of social history. They tell of economic highs and lows, of political progression, of technological advancement and social trends. Eating, in its necessity, is universal; through this commonality, the menu reflects popular culture in a way that no other medium can.

But the menu as we know it, especially in restaurants, has been an evolutionary process. Although the existence of menus can be traced back to tenth-century China, the first printed and displayed lists of edible offerings appeared in Paris in the mid-eighteenth century; at this stage, such records were more rough guides to the dishes that were likely to be put in front of you, eaten family style with other diners, rather than evocative descriptions of possibility. Furthermore, restaurants, in their early stages, were not seen as the preserve of the cultured, curious or wealthy, but more as a last resort for those away from home – that is, until the advent of the French Revolution. According to historian Rebecca L. Spang, in her book *The Invention of the Restaurant: Paris and Modern Gastronomic Culture*, dining out options didn't take an elegant turn until the chefs of the aristocracy found themselves out of work, and the resulting emergent middle classes had more money, less time and stronger inclination to have meals prepared for them. This, you could say, is at the core of the historical function of a menu – the first instance of how a record of what people ate held a light up to economic and social change. While bills of fare had been commonplace at private events, where, up until the mid-nineteenth century, dishes were presented on a communal table all at once, towards the end of the eighteenth century and beginning of the nineteenth century, daily offerings appeared on chalkboard signs – the translation being 'a la carte'. Fast forward just a few years, and the menu became somewhat more flamboyant, both in concept and structure. With the arrival of high-end hotels at the

These and following pages: Menu cards and covers from the collections of the British Library

A LONDRES
MAISON PRUNIER
St. James's Restaurant Ltd
72 St. James's Street
Telephone Regent 1373-1374

MENU
NO COVER CHARGED
(AUCUN PLAT N'EST SERVI POUR DEUX)

A PARIS
MAISON PRUNIER
9, Rue Duphot, Paris-1ᵉʳ
Traktir—16, Av. Victor Hugo-16
– OPEN AS USUAL

COQUILLAGES ET HUITRES

COQUILLAGES

Bigorneaux ....la portion	9d.
Moules Parquées........la douz.	1/-
Little Neck Clams petits ,,	4/-
Little Neck Clams gros ,,	7/-

POTTED SHRIMPS............... 2/3

COCKTAILS

Crevette Cocktail................	2/6
Crabe Cocktail....................	2/6
Langoustine Cocktail..........	3/-
Oyster Cocktail...................	3/6

HUITRES FRANCAISES

Portugaises...............	la douz.	4/-
Belon petites...............	,,	7/6
Belon supérieures........	,,	9/6
Armoricaines extra......	,,	11/-
Marennes vertes petites	,,	6/6
Marennes vertes supérieures	,,	9/6
Marennes vertes extra..	,,	10/6
L'Assiette Saintongeaise	...	3/-

(See full explanations on other page.)

LE PLATEAU PRUNIER

Petit Sandwich de Caviar de Saumon	
Petite Coquille salade de Crabe....	
Petite Coquille Moules au Curry	2/9
Petite coquille, sauce verte........	
Fine Bouche de Saumon Fumé......	

OEUFS

Œufs Lucullus................ 3/-

POTAGES

Bisque de Homard............	2/6
Clam Chowder................	3/6
Potage de Fruits de Mer....	4/-

HUITRES ANGLAISES

Brittany petites............	la douz.	6/-
Brittany supérieures....	,,	8/6
Natives Petites........	,,	7/6
Natives supérieures	,,	9/6
Natives extra.............	,,	11/-

BOUQUET............la portion 2/6

FUMAISONS, CAVIAR

Truite fumée..................	2/6
Saumon fumé..................	2/9
Caviar de Saumon.... la cuiller....	2/6
Caviar Pressé..................	2/6
Caviar Russe Sevruga (New Catch)	7/-
Caviar Russe Oscietre....(1939)	9/-

Omelette au Caviar............ 3/9

Crème de Maïs................	2/6
Soupe à l'Oignon gratinée....	2/6

NOS SPECIALITES

Huitres Frites........ les 3	2/6
,, au Gratin...... ,,	2/6
,, sur croûton.... ,,	2/6
,, à l'Américaine ,,	2/6
,, en Brochette.. ,,	2/6
Potage aux Huitres........	5/6
Variété Prunier (6 oysters)	5/-
Potage de Fruits de Mer	4/-
Clams à la Vapeur	4/6

Œuf en Gelée................ 1/9

Consommé aux Diablotins....	1/9
Soupe aux Moules..........	2/6

POISSONS

Le Poisson du Chef ....See "TODAY"
ESCARGOTS DE BOURGOGNE 3/6

Coquille de Moules Rémoulade	2/-	Crabe Dressé Mayonnaise.....	3/6	Truite en Gelée de Chablis...... 3/3
Crabe à la Mexicaine...........	2/6	Petit Homard Rémoulade......	4/-	Steak de Turbot Parisienne 3/6
		Langouste Mayonnaise........	4/6	

GRILLADE AU FENOUIL.... 3/6

Hareng Grillé, Sce. Moutarde....	2/-	Turbot au Four................	3/6	Bouillabaisse................ 3/6
Moules Marinière................	2/6	Sole Grillée....................	4/-	½ Homard Thermidor (1 per.) 4/6
Whitebaits Diablés..............	2/6	GRENOUILLES MURAT ½ douz.	4/6	Homard Grillé................ 4/6
Raie au beurre Noir	3/-	Pilaff de Moules au Curry....	3/6	Homard Américaine........... 5/-
St. Jacques Prunier...............	3/-	Pilaff de Crabe Américaine..	4/-	Homard Newburg............ 5/6
Truite Grenobloise..............	3/3	Pilaff de Langoustine Valencienne	4/6	Filets de Sole Prunier........ 4/6
		Pilaff de crevettes Newburg....	4/6	

ENTREES, GRILLADES ET ROTS

Le Plat du Gourmet...... "See TODAY"

Côtes d'Agneau................	3/6	Pilaff de Volaille au Curry...	3/6	Entrecôte Minute 3/9
Côte de Mouton ou Veau	3/6	½ Poularde au Riz Suprême (2 pers)	9/-	Tournedos Beurre d'Anchois... 4/6
Rognons Grillés Vert - Pré....	3/6	Poulet Maryland....(2 pers.)	9/-	Filet Boston (6 Huitres)...... 6/6

(Toutes les Grillades sont garnies Pommes Bataille)

GIBIER

Bécasse Flambée................	10/6	Noisette de Venaison, Sce. Poivrade	4/-	Civet de Lièvre.............. 3/6
Bécassine Liégeoise.............	4/6	Canard Sauvage au Porto.....	12/-	Râble Lièvre, Purée de Marrons 9/-

FROIDS

Langue.............................	2/6	Terrine de Lièvre.............	3/-	Poulet, la cuisse............ 3/6
Jambon d'York.................	2/6	Boeuf Mode en Gelée.........	3/-	Poulet, l'Aile................ 4/-
		Foie Gras à la Gelée de Porto	4/6	Mayonnaise de Volaille St. James's 4/-

LEGUMES

Haricots Verts au Beurre	2/-			Petits Pois à la Française.... 2/-
Endives Flamandes.............	2/-	Green Corn on Cob...........	2/-	Champignons Grillés Sur Toast 2/6

Salade de Saison: 1/3 — Salade Panachée 1/6 — Salade m.c.b. 1/6 — Salade de Légumes 2/-

FROMAGES

Cheddar, Cheshire 1/- Gruyère, Petit Suisse, Stilton 1/3 Camembert, Pont l'Eveque, Brie, Roquefort 1/6

ENTREMETS ET DESSERTS

Pôt de Crème; Chocolat, Vanille	1/6	Glace Vanille ou Fraise avec		Soufflé aux Marrons.......... 3/6
Fruits Rafraîchis au Marasquin	2/6	Gauffrettes Bretonnes	2/-	Crêpes à l'Orange............ 3/6
Ananas frais au Rhum.........	2/6	Mousse Glacée au Rhum ,, ,,	2/3	Poire Flambée à la Mirabelle 3/6
		Mousse Glacée Chocolat ,, ,,	2/3	
		Coupe Jack ,, ,,	2/6	

FRUITS DE SAISON

CAFE FILTRE 1/-   CAFE DECAFEINE 1/3   Grape Fruit 1/6

Open on Sundays for LUNCH at 12-30 and DINNER as usual – 7 p.m.
Starting from Sunday, 7th. January

"TOUT CE QUI VIENT DE LA MER — EVERYTHING COMING FROM THE SEA"

beginning of the nineteenth century, menus in Europe and North America became more of a showcase, adorned with illustrations and offering a wide variety of choice, as opposed to a non-negotiable series of dishes. From this springboard, the menu has become everything from a creative portfolio to a statement of ethical intent – think Picasso's illustrations for his regular haunt in Barcelona versus London's first vegetarian restaurant, frequented by household names from the hippy movement of the 1960s.

But what about menus outside of restaurants? Typically, these kinds of menus offer more of an insight into political and social narratives. A menu celebrating Indian Independence Day in Delhi, for example (page 103) speaks volumes about the country's complex past, and perhaps hints at an even more complex cultural identity that would exist far into the future. As such, the dinner menu for Churchill's birthday during the Tehran conference of 1943 with allies Stalin and Roosevelt in its content can be seen as a display of diplomacy, or an indication of the very human and nuanced power struggles that exist on both a micro and macro scale.

And, there is the more abstract concept of 'the menu' – food and drink that, from humble or radical beginnings, has become commonplace on kitchen and restaurant tables the world over. Would the childhood indulgence of dehydrated ice cream have been as romanticised had it not been for NASA technology allowing both humans and their sustenance to travel in space? And, had it not been for the marketing prowess of US company Heinz in the early nineteenth century, would baked beans be as ubiquitous in the UK as they are today?

In this book, 250 years of history is explored through food and drink, and, just like the accompanying visuals, what can be found is abundantly varied and rich. In honour of the now-traditional menu format, it is divided into three sections – Starters, Mains and Desserts. The premise is simple: to start, we assess beginning points, innovations and pioneers, from Escoffier's groundbreaking menu at The Ritz to the introduction of frozen TV dinners in middle-class American homes. These are menus that are defined by their point of difference, and are divided into three sections – Menu Firsts, Food Inventions and Iconic Menus. Turn to page 15 to find out more. Next, we delve into Mains, for menus that either reflect or embody important social and political changes in European and North American history. These happenings range from Christmas dinner in the First World War trenches and the introduction of free school dinners for primary school children in the UK, to the publication of the first cookbook with colour photographs. They are divided as such into three categories: Meals that Made History, Social Changes that Made Menus and A History of Cookbooks. The final flourish, of course, is Desserts, whereby things become more jubilant and sorrowful in equal measure, much like the end of a meal. The focus of this chapter is extravagance, drama and creativity: meals, events or quirky eating habits of the rich and famous that have gone down in history for their social, political or cultural significance. Here, Famous Feasts, Food in the Arts and Last Meals are explored, from lavish parties of the last Russian Tsar to Ernest Hemingway's classic camping menu and President Nixon's last lunch in the White House.

While the menus you see in the following pages are categorised and ordered chronologically, any sense of a linear narrative ends here; this is more a selection of snapshots of history intended to pique interest, amuse and surprise, rather than a cohesive yet plodding journey through culinary history. Much like a good restaurant menu, the intention of this book is to present a little of the unknown, a more focused expression of the familiar, and a few twists on classics. How else could one connect eating dogs and cats during the Paris siege to the wedding breakfast of Elvis Presley? From infamous feasts to 'secret' menus, from wartime tea tables to presidential lunches, the menus here, however varied, all carry the weight of historical significance. A menu, it seems, is far more complex and far reaching in its relevance than the subsequent meal that is placed in front of us.

STARTERS

On a restaurant menu, the starters section has two functions: the first, to stimulate appetite, and the second, to set a precedent for the main event. In this selection of historic menus, the aim is to do just that. From the creation of the Martini and the now ubiquitous fast food restaurant, to strawberries and cream at Wimbledon and Escoffier's first offerings at The Ritz, this chapter highlights the very best of these firsts. The following menus pique interest, define social and historical context, and present pioneers that later became icons. Whether it's a simple technological advancement that led to the mass production of previously luxury – and now commonplace – items, revolutionary ways to eat on the move, or original incarnations of culinary cultural icons, these menus are historical starting points of journeys that have long since continued.

Curry, Curry, Curry.

R. BANKS,

2 & 3, Green Street, Leicester Square,

SERVES A REAL INDIAN CURRY

Daily from 12 to 3.

Tennyson wrote of the "Cock," and
Their plump head waiter,
Where often he used to resort
At the hour of five by his indicator
To indulge in a pint of old port.

I write of the Crown
Where men of renown,
To Banks' like good citizens hurry,
To lodge there their cash,
And receive not a hash,
But a luncheon of Real Indian Curry.

Friday, the Gt. Madras authority on Curry advises,
Thoom Curry Khana Koo Mungtha Banks Sab Ka pass goue.

Wines, Spirits and Malt Liquors of the highest character.

Nov 5 1886

W. STRAKER, Printer, Ludgate Hill, E.C.

Advert for a nineteenth-century curry house, London

MENU FIRSTS

Popcorn in the cinema, fish and chips on a rainy beach, farmers' markets, roadside fry-ups and three-course menus — sometimes, things are so culturally ingrained that it never occurs to one to think about where they came from. Here, discover exactly how and why some menus have helped to shape a shared social history.

1808	Service à la Russe in Paris
1810	The UK's First Indian Restaurant
1860	Joseph Malin's Fish and Chips
1868	Dining by Rail
1877	Tennis Meets Strawberries and Cream
1915	The Life of a Box of Chocolates
1919	The Women's Institute's Farmers' Markets
1930	How Food Reached US Cinemas
1958	Saturday Night Takeaways
1958	How We All Came to Love Little Chef

BILLS OF FARE.

JANVIER.   243

DÎNER, 60 COUVERTS—SERVICE À LA RUSSE.
MENU.
Servi par six, dix sur chaque plat.

BUFFET SÉPARÉ.

Vermuth, Absinthe,	Canapés de crevettes (777)	Salade d'anchois (772)
Kümmel, Sherry	Gelée de canneberges (598)	Rhubarbe à la crème (3204)
	Thon mariné (831)	Radis (808)
	Olives (800)	Caviar (778)
Chablis	60 plats d'huîtres sur coquilles (803)	

POTAGES (3 SOUPIÈRES).

Amontillado   Consommé Colbert aux œufs pochés (225)   Bisque de homard (205)

HORS-D'ŒUVRE (3 PLATS DE CHAQUE).

Timbales à la Talleyrand (988)   Palmettes à la Perrier (922)

POISSONS (3 PLATS DE CHAQUE).

Haut Sauterne   Flétan à la Coligny (1168)   Filets de soles, Rochelaise (1276)

RELEVÉS (3 PLATS DE CHAQUE).

Batailly   Dinde à la Française (2029)   Selle d'agneau à la Chancelière (1739)

ENTRÉES (3 PLATS DE CHAQUE).

Champagne   Filets de volaille à la Certosa (1836)   Côtelettes de tétras à la Ségard (2259)
Pommery Sec
Homard à la Rougemont (1041)   Chaudfroid de cailles à la Baudy (2459)

RÔTS (3 PLATS DE CHAQUE).

Perdreaux truffés (2100)   Poularde au cresson (1996)

LÉGUMES (3 PLATS DE CHAQUE).

Château   Céleri à la moelle (2721)   Petits pois fins à la Parisienne (2745)
La Rose

ENTREMETS SUCRÉS (CHAUDS) (3 PLATS DE CHAQUE).

Brioches St. Marc (3006)   Pouding à la Benvenuto (3092)

ENTREMETS SUCRÉS (FROIDS) (3 PLATS DE CHAQUE).

Vin de Paille   Gelée aux fruits (3 plats) (3187)
Gaufres brisselets à la crème framboisée (3223)
60 Glaces variées (3538)

FLANCS.

2 Chariots garnis de pommes d'api (3632)
Une brouette garnie de fleurs sur socle (3638)

CONTRE FLANCS.

Deux étagères garnies de bonbons, marrons glacés et Victorias (3379)
8 Tambours garnis de petits fours (3364)   Macarons (3379)
Africains (3364)   Bouchées de dames (3376)

SEIZE BOUTS DE TABLE.

4 Corbeilles de fruits frais (3699)   4 Compotiers de fruits secs (3699)
4 Fromages (3697)   4 Compotes de pommes (3686)
Café (3701)

A Russian-style menu from Charles Ranhofer's book *The Epicurean*, published in 1894

1808

SERVICE À LA RUSSE IN PARIS

IF ONE WERE TO GUESS the origination of sequential dining – i.e., each dish being served separately, as opposed to all at once – it's likely that the answer would be France, or maybe at a push, Italy. But how many would say Russia?

The shape of menus in Western Europe is in actual fact a consequence of Russian Ambassador Alexander Kurakin's service in Paris from 1808–10. Kukarin, known as the 'Diamond Prince' on account of his elaborate wardrobe and even more elaborate banquets, hosted his dinners Russian style – that is, serving guests dishes one course at a time, so that they may appreciate the qualities of each, along with cutlery for each course, and a name card at each table setting. At this time, *service à la Française*, whereby every dish, be it starter, main or dessert, arrived on the table at once, was the done thing, but perhaps unsurprisingly, once sequential dining became popular among the elite, the style spread. The practice eventually reached England in the latter part of the century, even making it into *Mrs Beeton's Book of Household Management* (1861).

This menu, an example of the *service à la Russe* style exemplified by Ranhofer in *The Epicurean*, shows a dinner of an almost overwhelming number of courses, the likes of which were *de rigueur* on a high-society dinner table: caviar, lobster bisque, truffled partridge and candied chestnuts.

An example of a *service à la Russe* table setting from *A Manual of Domestic Economy* by J. H. Walsh, 1874

Portrait of Sake Dean Mahomed, c.1810

1810

THE UK'S FIRST INDIAN RESTAURANT

HOOKAH

·

MEAT DRESSED WITH THE BEST SPICES OF ARABIA

·

RICE

IT'S LIKELY THAT THE towns in the UK today without an Indian restaurant or take-away shop could be counted on one hand. And while the surge in popularity and ubiquity can certainly be credited to the Bangladeshi immigrants of the 1970s, the first-ever Indian restaurant was established by Sake Dean Mahomed, a Bengali entrepreneur and captain in the East India Company, who bears another credit to his name: he was latterly the Prince Regent's barber.

Hindoostane Coffee House opened in 1810 near Portman Square, Marylebone, London, and while it's true that Indian-style food had been served in homes and restaurants since the previous century, however sparingly, this was the first establishment to be Indian owned and run. All that's known of the food served at Hindoostane Coffee House was that dishes were lightly spiced, to appeal to palates unfamiliar with the flavours, and served with rice; as described in *The Epicure's Almanack* of 1815, 'dishes were dressed with curry powder, rice, cayenne and the best spices of Arabia', surrounded by the aroma of hookah pipes. It's said that Mahomed's diners were most commonly the British who had returned from India and diplomats from India who were stationed in London, although the latter would most likely have been unfamiliar with the Anglicised versions of regional food.

Sadly, the restaurant closed within four years. However, the legacy of this early culinary pioneer remains – you'll even find a green plaque at the restaurant's location.

An advert for fish and chips in *Everybody* magazine, 1957

1860

JOSEPH MALIN'S FISH AND CHIPS

BATTERED COD

·

CHIPPED POTATOES

·

MUSHY PEAS

IT'S HARD TO IMAGINE a time when there wasn't a chippy on every city street corner, but, believe it or not, the ingredients of this so-called icon of British culture weren't inextricably linked together until the 1860s. Concrete evidence of the first to make the connection remains elusive, however; the first 'chip' shop is believed to have originated in Oldham, Greater Manchester, where a blue plaque marks the spot that 'chipped' potatoes were first sold in this manner. But the combination of the two in one fryer is widely credited to Joseph Malin, a London-based Jewish immigrant from Central Europe, whose first shop was in Cleveland Street, Stepney. It then moved to Old Ford Road in Bow, and was run by his grandson until as late as the 1960s.

Most likely, fried fish was an import from the Jewish community of Portugal in the late eighteenth century – it's even mentioned in Dickens' works, such as *Oliver Twist* and *A Tale of Two Cities* – while potatoes prepared in this style are almost certainly of Irish origin. When it comes to accompaniments of more recent years, though, regional preferences play a strong part. Mushy peas are most popular in the north of England and the Midlands, and the same can be said for curry sauce and gravy. And a final note – if you're eating fish and chips in the south, you expect to find the fish skin-on – a somewhat controversial action north of London.

TOUR OF THE PRESIDENT THROUGH THE NORTHWEST.

Breakfast

FRESH FRUIT

ROLLED OATS WITH CREAM

BROILED FRESH MACKEREL

SIRLOIN STEAK, PLAIN, MUSHROOMS OR TOMATO SAUCE

HAM   BREAKFAST BACON

LAMB CHOPS

FRIED COUNTRY SAUSAGE

BROILED TEAL DUCK

EGGS—   BOILED   FRIED   SCRAMBLED

OMELETTES—PLAIN, WITH HAM, PARSLEY, JELLY OR RUM

POTATOES—   BAKED   FRIED   STEWED IN CREAM

GREEN TEA   ENGLISH BREAKFAST TEA

COFFEE   MILK   COCOA

GRIDDLE CAKES, MAPLE SYRUP

CORN MUFFINS   TOAST   HOT ROLLS

Pullman Dining Car Service.
En Route, September 21, 1902.

Breakfast menu for the 'Tour of the President Through the Northwest', Pullman dining-car service, 21 September 1902

1868

DINING BY RAIL

EATING ON THE MOVE in the 1800s was a far cry from the world of miniature plastic wine bottles and packet sandwiches that we live in today. Dining on board a train was as much about the elegance of the experience as it was the practicalities of cutting journey times by avoiding lunch stops.

The 'dining car' concept was established in the US in 1868 by the Pullman Company, manufacturers of railroad cars; before this, long distance journeys were broken up by stops at 'roadhouses', which served basic food and drinks, at best, prioritising value and practicality over luxury. Before too long, cars were opening on all the major routes across the country, with each dining car more luxurious than the last.

Meals weren't served on trains in the UK until 1879, when a Pullman restaurant car, imported from Detroit, ran on the Great Northern Railway between London King's Cross and Leeds, and it was, unsurprisingly, given the undertaking, a first-class service. All food was prepared on board by a chef, with the entire car comprising, according to the *Illustrated London News*, 'a dining salon in the middle, a kitchen behind, and a smoking room in front, with steward's pantry, ladies dressing room, gentlemen's lavatory, cupboards and stoves'.

But back to America: this extravagant breakfast menu, served exclusively for Theodore Roosevelt's campaign tour of the Northwest to bolster votes for Republican candidates, highlights how the Pullman Company elevated the service on both sides of the pond, with cooked-to-order sirloin steak, eggs, duck, and griddle cakes with maple syrup.

Menu from the Great Northern Railway dining-car service, UK

Dining car on the Pacific Railway, in the US, from Charles Lucas's private collection, c.1877–9

Coverage of Wimbledon in *Throne and Country* magazine, 16 June 1909

1877

TENNIS MEETS STRAWBERRIES AND CREAM

PIMM'S
·
CUCUMBER SANDWICHES
·
STRAWBERRIES AND CREAM

OF COURSE, THIS CLASSIC food combination has a longer history than the British sporting event that it's now so widely associated with – a stalwart on the banqueting table of the Tudors, strawberries and cream supposedly became popular after its inception in the kitchens of Hampton Court Palace in the early 1500s. The dish itself is much discussed, but the exact details of when strawberries and cream became a hit with the crowds at Wimbledon are less certain. The first Wimbledon Tennis Championship took place in 1877, when, according to several food historians, strawberries were a very much in-vogue, luxury item – at their seasonal peak in early July – and all evidence points to this dish being served to the 200 or more attendees of the inaugural tournament. Fast forward to 1954, and an article in the *Coventry Evening Telegraph* marvelled at how the popularity and associated glamour of the competition had grown in the previous 50 years, examples of this being 'pressmen everywhere' and 'strawberry-and-cream teas on the lawns outside'. However it happened, the dessert has become so inextricably linked with experience of the tournament, that in 2017, 33 tonnes of strawberries were consumed.

Cadbury's Milk Tray advert in *Everybody* magazine, 1957

1915

THE LIFE OF A BOX OF CHOCOLATES

PERFECT PRALINE

·

HAZELNUT SWIRL

·

STRAWBERRY TEMPTATION

·

LIME CORDIAL

·

EXOTIC CHARM

ALTHOUGH NOW IT'S DIFFICULT to imagine one of the UK's most famous boxes of chocolate without a vision of the iconic 'Milk Tray Man' from 1968–2003, Cadbury's have been making this selection box since 1915. The name for the box derived from the manner in which chocolate was presented to customers at this time; arranged on trays, chocolates were sold loose and packed into boxes – a luxury, and far from commonplace. Starting with the tray presentation format, Cadbury's preselected chocolates in a manageable half pound size, complete with pretty purple packaging, became an instant hit. Being both decadent yet comparatively affordable for the middle classes, chocolates became the gift of choice for social occasions, and by the mid 1930s, Milk Tray was the most popular chocolate box in the UK – a noteworthy rival being Rowntree's Black Magic selection. Of course, over time, flavours have changed, but there are always the enduring favourites – Perfect Praline, Hazelnut Swirl and Strawberry Temptation, to name three – while flavours such as Lime Cordial and Exotic Charm, Cadbury's interpretation of Turkish delight, ceased to exist.

Trugs of produce, Eastbourne WI market, c.1935

1919

THE WOMEN'S INSTITUTE'S FARMERS' MARKETS

SEASONAL VEGETABLES
·
VICTORIA SPONGE
·
APRICOT TART

THE WOMEN'S INSTITUTE, OR WI as it's more commonly known, is unique in its appeal as both an icon of the past while also playing a vital and progressive role in the present and future. When this community-led organisation was formed in the UK in 1915, the purpose was to re-energise rural areas in the depths of the First World War, encouraging women to produce food and maintain the farming industry during the years of conscription. As part of this drive, the WI organised local markets where women could bring produce from their gardens and smallholdings, the aim being to sell surplus food to the local community. The first such market was held in Lewes, East Sussex, 1919, and at its most productive point, had up to 23 different stalls. Members sold everything from seasonal vegetables and flowers to eggs, butter, cream, cakes, jams and preservatives produced at their smallholdings, with the initiative eventually opening up to local farmers and ex-servicemen. Popular recipes of the day included Victoria sponge, apricot tart and fruit cake. In the *West Sussex Gazette*, the event was listed as an 'opportunity for young women'; as this initiative continued to support the local economy during both the Depression and the Second World War, and beyond, it's safe to say it's evolved into an opportunity for the whole community.

Man buying snacks at the concession stand, US, date unknown

1930

HOW FOOD REACHED AMERICAN CINEMAS

POPCORN

·

SODA

·

CANDY

TODAY, POPCORN IS SYNONOMOUS with movies the world over, but the reason as to why we snack during a film has less to do with hunger, and more to do with the economic benefits to theatre owners during America's Great Depression in the 1930s. While the first ever 'film' was played to a paying audience in Paris, 1895, by the Lumière brothers – arguably the godfathers of the film industry – it wasn't until some 30 years later that popcorn came on the scene.

Up to the mid-1920s, all films were silent, with subtitles. Not only did this make for a hear-a-pin-drop atmosphere, but it also prohibited most from enjoying the picture, given the literacy rate of the lower classes. But with the advent of so-called 'talkies', cinema suddenly became accessible, and as a result, business boomed. Popcorn was already a popular snack in the US, but, as frivolity took a hit with the economic downturn, cinema owners found a way to increase profit with very little investment, and so food – popcorn, soda and candy – became very much part of the experience, whether being sold by independent sellers strolling the aisles, or in the form of a stand in the foyer.

APPETISERS

1. Mixed Appetiser *(Served 2)* £7.50
   (Includes Spare Ribs, Seaweed, Sesame Prawn on Toast, Spring Rolls & Fried Chicken Wings)
2. Spare Ribs in BBQ sauce £4.80
3. Spare Ribs with Spices & Chilli 🌶 £4.80
4. Capital Spare Ribs with Fruity Sauce £4.80
5. Dry Spare Ribs *(Served with Lemon)* £4.80
6. Deep Fried Chicken with Spices & Chilli 🌶 £4.20
7. Deep Fried Chicken Wings with Sweet Chilli Dip *(6)* 🌶 £3.60
8. Butterfly King Prawns with Breadcrumbs £4.80
9. Sesame Prawn on Toast £2.80
10. Crispy King Prawns with Spices & Chilli 🌶 £4.80
11. Crispy Squid with Spices & Chilli 🌶 £4.80
12. Grilled Dumplings *(4)* £3.00
    (Vinegar & Ginger Dip)
13. Satay Chicken with Peanut Sauce *(3 skewers)* £3.60
14. Satay Beef with Peanut Sauce ... £3.80
    (3 skewers)
15. Crispy Seaweed £3.00
16. Crispy Won Ton with Sweet & Sour Sauce £3.00
17. Spring Rolls *(2)* £2.20
18. Mini Vegetable Spring Rolls *(8)* ... £2.00
19. Vegetable Samosas *(8)* £2.00
20. Prawn Crackers £1.50
21. Crispy Aromatic Duck ...... *Quarter* £7.50
    (Served with Pancakes, ... *Half* £13.50
    Cucumber, Spring Onions & Hoisin Sauce)
22. Crispy Pork £6.00
    (Served with Pancakes, Cucumber, Spring Onions & Hoisin Sauce)

SOUPS

23. Chicken & Sweetcorn Soup £2.00
24. 'Crabmeat' & Sweetcorn Soup £2.20
25. Chicken & Noodle Soup £2.00
26. Chicken & Mushroom Soup £2.00
27. Mixed Vegetable Soup £2.00
28. Hot & Sour Soup £2.20
29. 'Tom Yum' Thai Prawn Soup £2.50
30. 'Tom Yum' Thai Chicken Soup £2.50

CHICKEN DISHES

31. Crispy Shredded Chicken with Chilli Sauce 🌶🌶 ... £4.50
32. Chicken with Cashew Nuts £4.50
33. Chicken 'Chinese Style' *(with a Bed of Beansprouts)*.. £4.20
34. Chicken with Ginger & Spring Onions £4.20
35. Chicken with Mushrooms £4.20
36. Chicken with Green Peppers & Black Bean Sauce 🌶 £4.20
37. Chicken with Mushrooms & Black Bean Sauce 🌶 £4.20
38. Chicken with Bamboo Shoots & Water Chestnuts £4.20
39. Chicken with Pineapple £4.20
40. Chicken in Satay Sauce 🌶 £4.20
41. Chicken 'Szechuan Style' 🌶🌶 £4.20
42. Chicken in Lemon Sauce £4.20
43. Kung Po Chilli Chicken 🌶🌶 £4.20

DUCK DISHES

44. Roast Duck 'Chinese' Style £4.80
    (with a Bed of Beansprouts)
45. Duck with Cashew Nuts £4.80
46. Duck with Ginger & Spring Onions £4.80
47. Duck with Mushrooms in Oyster Sauce £4.80
48. Duck with Green Peppers & Black Bean Sauce 🌶 £4.80
49. Duck with Pineapple £4.80
50. Duck in Orange Sauce £4.80
51. Duck in Plum Sauce £4.80

MEAT DISHES

52. Crispy Shredded Beef with Chilli Sauce 🌶🌶 .... £4.50^^
53. Beef with Cashew Nuts £4.30
54. Beef with Ginger and Spring Onions £4.20
55. Beef with Mushrooms in Oyster Sauce £4.20
56. Beef with Green Peppers & Black Bean Sauce 🌶 £4.20
57. Beef with Mushrooms & Black Bean Sauce 🌶 £4.20
58. Beef in Satay Sauce 🌶 £4.20
59. Beef 'Szechuan Style' 🌶🌶 £4.20
60. Beef with Tomato £4.20
61. Lamb with Ginger & Spring Onions £4.70
62. Lamb with Green Peppers & Black Bean Sauce 🌶 £4.70

Lucky House Takeaway, Peterborough, UK, date unknown

1958

SATURDAY NIGHT TAKEAWAYS

SWEET AND SOUR CHICKEN

·

CHOP SUEY

·

CHIPS

THE BRITISH HAVE LONG had a love affair with Chinese food, supposedly dating back to the late nineteenth century, when restaurants and supermarkets began opening in port cities such as Liverpool and London as a result of maritime trade, with the country's first 'Chinatown' appearing in Limehouse in the capital's East End around 1910. The number of restaurants began to steadily increase after the Second World War, firstly as a result of people relocating from Hong Kong, and secondly, because the British government's stand against Mao Zedong's Communist regime left embassy workers stranded in the capital. But it wasn't until 1958 that the concept of takeaway Chinese food was born.

As the story goes, the son of Chung Koon, one of London's first Chinese restaurant owners, opened The Lotus House in Bayswater, west London, and the food became so popular that customers who were unable to secure a table asked to take food home. The menu at this point was heavily adapted to suit the British palate, including all the favourites from traditional English menus, such as steak, omelettes, chips and even a mixed grill, but also offered chop suey (a Westernised noodle dish) and sweet and sour chicken and pork. Opening around 11.30 pm, when pubs were closing, and offering affordable food, Chinese restaurants and takeaways soon began springing up across the country.

Little Chef motorway map, 1987

1958

HOW WE ALL CAME TO LOVE LITTLE CHEF

BAKED BEANS ON TOAST

·

GAMMON STEAK WITH EGG AND PINEAPPLE

·

FRUIT COCKTAIL WITH ICE CREAM

MUCH LIKE IT'S US fast-food counterparts, Little Chef, a chain of roadside restaurants that opened in the UK in 1958, was a reflection of changing social trends; the building of motorways across the country, a rise in two-income families, and a desire for convenience created a perfect storm for the expansion of the chain. Although roadside inns have existed for hundreds of years, the 'diner' concept was something that Little Chef owner Sam Alper took from the US, and within ten years, there were 25 restaurants located on A-roads across the UK.

For a while, Little Chef had very little competition – McDonald's didn't open its first site here until 1974, followed by Burger King in 1976, and neither at this stage were aiming for on-the-move clientele. The first restaurant was, in fact, a small caravan just outside of Reading. Alper had previously been the designer and manufacturer of Sprite caravans, which had helped him to see a gap in the market for feeding hungry families travelling for their holidays. Early menus included 'traveller's snacks' such as cheeseburgers, baked beans on toast, gammon steak with egg and pineapple, liver with bacon and onions, steak with onion rings and chips from the griddle, and fruit cocktail with ice cream and pancakes with sugared raisins as a sweet option. The iconic 'Jubilee' pancake, filled with cherries and vanilla ice cream, first appeared on the menu in 1976, while the equally popular 'Olympic' breakfast – bacon, sausage, eggs, mushrooms, sautéed potatoes, grilled tomatoes, hash browns, baked beans and fried bread – was a latecomer in 1994.

Although Little Chef's fortunes turned and its last outlet closed in 2018, its legacy will forever be bound with the phrase 'are we nearly there yet?'

1 Double-Double, French Fries, and Medium Drink	$7.60 +tax	
2 Cheeseburger, French Fries, and Medium Drink	$6.40 +tax	
3 Hamburger, French Fries, and Medium Drink	$6.10 +tax	

DOUBLE-DOUBLE® *Double Meat Double Cheese* $3.95

CHEESEBURGER $2.75

HAMBURGER $2.45

Fresh FRENCH FRIES $1.85

SHAKES *Chocolate Strawberry Vanilla* $2.50

NUTRITION INFORMATION AVAILABLE UPON REQUEST

COKE *Classic or Diet*
ROOT BEER
DR PEPPER
SEVEN-UP
LEMONADE *Pink or Light*
ICED TEA

SM	MED	LG	X-LG
$1.65	$1.80	$2.00	$2.20

MILK $.99
HOT COCOA 8 oz. $1.80
COFFEE $1.35

IN-N-OUT BURGER

OPEN 10:30 a.m. to 1:00 a.m.
............Fri. and Sat. until 1:30 a.m.

In-N-Out Burger drive-thru menu, US, date unknown

FOOD INVENTIONS

At the heart of many a good idea is convenience, and this section, dedicated to innovation, explores everything from freezer food to the world's most famous cocktail. When it comes to eating, it seems creativity isn't limited to just what's on the plate — or in the glass — in front of you.

1832   The World's Most Famous Chocolate Cake

1887   The First Taste of a Martini

1901   Why Beanz Meanz Heinz

1947   Drive-through Dining

1953   TV Dinners

1958   Noodles in an Instant

1980   Supermarket Sandwiches

2011   A History of Ice Cream in the UK

Hotel Sacher's famous cake, presented in its signature wooden box

1832

THE WORLD'S MOST FAMOUS CHOCOLATE CAKE

SACHERTORTE
·
SPICED BUNDT CAKE
·
VIENNESE APPLE STRUDEL

THIS RICH CHOCOLATE CAKE with apricot jam is perhaps one of Austria's most famous exports, but contrary to popular belief, its appearance on menus was a slow and steady race. Sachertorte is commonly associated with the luxury Viennese hotel of the same name, its creation largely credited to chef Eduard Sacher, however, the first iterations of this dessert were made by Eduard's father, Franz.

In 1832, as a 16-year-old apprentice in the kitchen of Prince Wenzel von Metternich, Franz fudged it when the head chef was taken ill on the night of an important dinner, and the result was a crowd-pleaser that shaped the course of culinary history – eventually. It wasn't until his son, Eduard Sacher, by then a pastry chef, revisited his father's recipe that it became something of a sensation when it was put on the menu of the Hotel Sacher in 1876. The recipe remains exactly the same, and was a closely guarded secret until Eduard Sacher's grandson, Franz, sold the recipe to Demel Patisserie, resulting in a lengthy lawsuit and a ruling that only the Hotel Sacher could claim to have the original recipe. Demel had to be satisfied with the 'Original Eduard Sacher Torte'. The main difference between the two recipes is that in Sacher's case, the layer of jam is between two layers of the chocolate sponge, while in Demel's version the jam is on top of the sponge but under the chocolate covering.

Today, around 360,000 cakes are eaten each year, every one decorated with a chocolate stamp and served with whipped cream. But it's not the only original on the hotel menu; Sachertorte happily sits alongside a spiced Bundt cake and a Viennese apple strudel that have been served for more than 180 years.

Drinks

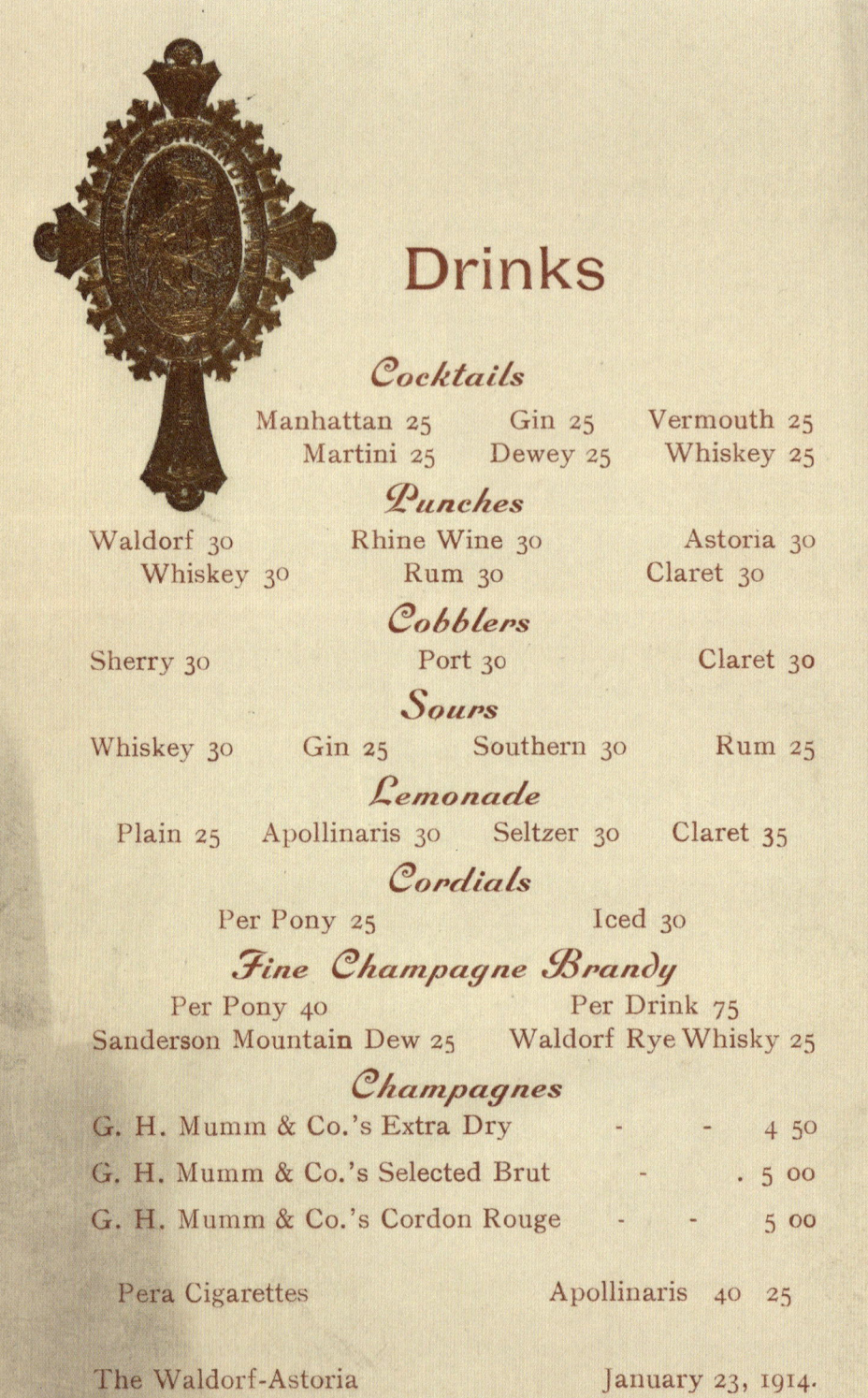

Cocktails

Manhattan 25　　Gin 25　　Vermouth 25
Martini 25　　Dewey 25　　Whiskey 25

Punches

Waldorf 30　　Rhine Wine 30　　Astoria 30
Whiskey 30　　Rum 30　　Claret 30

Cobblers

Sherry 30　　Port 30　　Claret 30

Sours

Whiskey 30　　Gin 25　　Southern 30　　Rum 25

Lemonade

Plain 25　　Apollinaris 30　　Seltzer 30　　Claret 35

Cordials

Per Pony 25　　Iced 30

Fine Champagne Brandy

Per Pony 40　　Per Drink 75
Sanderson Mountain Dew 25　　Waldorf Rye Whisky 25

Champagnes

G. H. Mumm & Co.'s Extra Dry　—　—　4 50

G. H. Mumm & Co.'s Selected Brut　—　. 5 00

G. H. Mumm & Co.'s Cordon Rouge　—　—　5 00

Pera Cigarettes　　　　Apollinaris 40 25

The Waldorf-Astoria　　　　January 23, 1914.

Drinks menu from the Waldorf-Astoria, US, 1914

1887

THE FIRST TASTE OF A MARTINI

UNFORTUNATELY, THE HISTORY OF this iconic cocktail, unlike its appearance, is anything but simple. While theories abound, it is safe to say, at the very least, that this was an American invention, most likely towards the end of the nineteenth century. Whether it was in a bar in San Francisco, California, or a hotel in New York is up for debate, but either way, the popularity of this drink has rarely waned since a version of it appeared in Jerry Thomas's *Bartender's Guide* in 1887.

Early versions of the martini were a sweeter affair: often half gin, half vermouth, and sometimes with a twist of lemon. It wasn't until the early twentieth century that the 'dry' martini became popular, and, ironically, established its base components during the Prohibition era, when moonshine became the dominant ingredient over harder-to-source vermouth. This, in turn, led to the martini making its journey to Europe, where US citizens opened American-style bars, and so old fashioneds, juleps and martinis, became popular the world over.

This menu from the Waldorf-Astoria in 1914 shows the martini to be an established favourite, alongside the Manhattan, a cocktail of whiskey, vermouth and bitters, believed to have originated from New York (of course) in the late 1800s.

BAKED IN REAL OVENS! — *That's Why*

Baked Beans are baked beans only when they're really baked—baked brown, baked tender, baked delicious, baked nutritious, baked as Heinz bakes them—in real ovens.

There's a big difference between beans that are not baked and beans that are. That is why the label cannot say "BAKED" unless the beans *are* baked.

Ask for *baked*. Look for *baked*. Serve *baked*—and you have the *baked bean* dish supreme—HEINZ.

WHEN IN PITTSBURGH BE SURE TO VISIT THE HEINZ KITCHENS · H. J. HEINZ COMPANY

Advert from the *Saturday Evening Post*, 1927

1901

WHY BEANZ MEANZ HEINZ

ON TOAST, IN A jacket potato, next to – but not touching – the egg on a fry-up: baked beans have become synonymous with British childhood home comforts. In light of that, the following facts may come as a surprise. Firstly, baked beans are an American product, initially imported from across the pond, and continued to be for 20 years, until Heinz set up a factory in the UK. Secondly, Heinz Baked Beans were originally billed as a luxury item, and went on sale for the first time in the high-end London department store, Fortnum & Mason in 1901.

In the Edwardian period, an 'English' breakfast was adopted by the middle classes as a family meal, as opposed to the Victorian perspective of the English breakfast as an outward display of luxury to guests. Being commonly available, baked beans joined other such easy-to-source ingredients – bacon, egg, black pudding – on the plate. The popularity of beans steadily grew, but it was really as a result of the Second World War that a tin of Heinz became a hero; while the brand's ketchup disappeared from shelves during this time because of sugar shortages, baked beans were championed as 'essential' by the Ministry of Food, and so were further embraced by all classes for everyday dining.

In this American advert from 1927, Heinz's unique selling point was the bean being baked home-style, meaning a superior flavour. Indeed, it wasn't until 2008 that they were rebranded to just 'Heinz Beanz' – according to Heinz, the reasons for this were two-fold: firstly, as a tribute to their iconic 'Beanz Meanz Heinz' campaign of the 1960s, and secondly, because the full title was a bit of a mouthful.

Illustration of an American ambassador serving baked beans to dignitaries from around the globe, *Puck* magazine, 1806

S ABROAD.
ne more baked beans, Princess. My wife cooked them herself.

In-N-Out Burger in Pasedena, California, US

1947

DRIVE-THROUGH DINING

HAMBURGER
·
CHEESEBURGER
·
FRIES
·
ROOT BEER

DRIVE-THROUGH RESTAURANTS, or 'drive-thrus', as they are commonly referred to, unsurprisingly originated in the USA; in the late 1940s and early 1950s, the car business was booming, more and more wives were working full-time jobs, and so food, along with family time, became more focused on speed and convenience. Ordering and picking up food through a window removed the need for getting out of the car, saving precious time – and thus, a way of life was created. It's reported that the first drive-through opened in 1947 at Red's Giant Hamburg in Springfield, Missouri, on the iconic Route 66. Though it was originally just a petrol station, the owner, Red Chaney, decided to branch out and sell hamburgers – which was just as well, as he used meat from his own small cattle herd to make them. The drive-through was so named because of a slip up with the size of the signage – 'hamburger' became 'hamburg' as a consequence.

Understandably, the craze caught on, and the California-based In-N-Out Burger opened as a 'Drive Thru' restaurant in 1948. The menu on opening day was simple: a hamburger, a cheeseburger, fries and a selection of soft drinks. Some 70 years later, the menu isn't that much more expansive, although an urban myth persists about a 'secret' menu at each of the 334 restaurants across the west coast of the US. This innovation coincided with the development of California's motorway network, and before too long, there were dozens of restaurants.

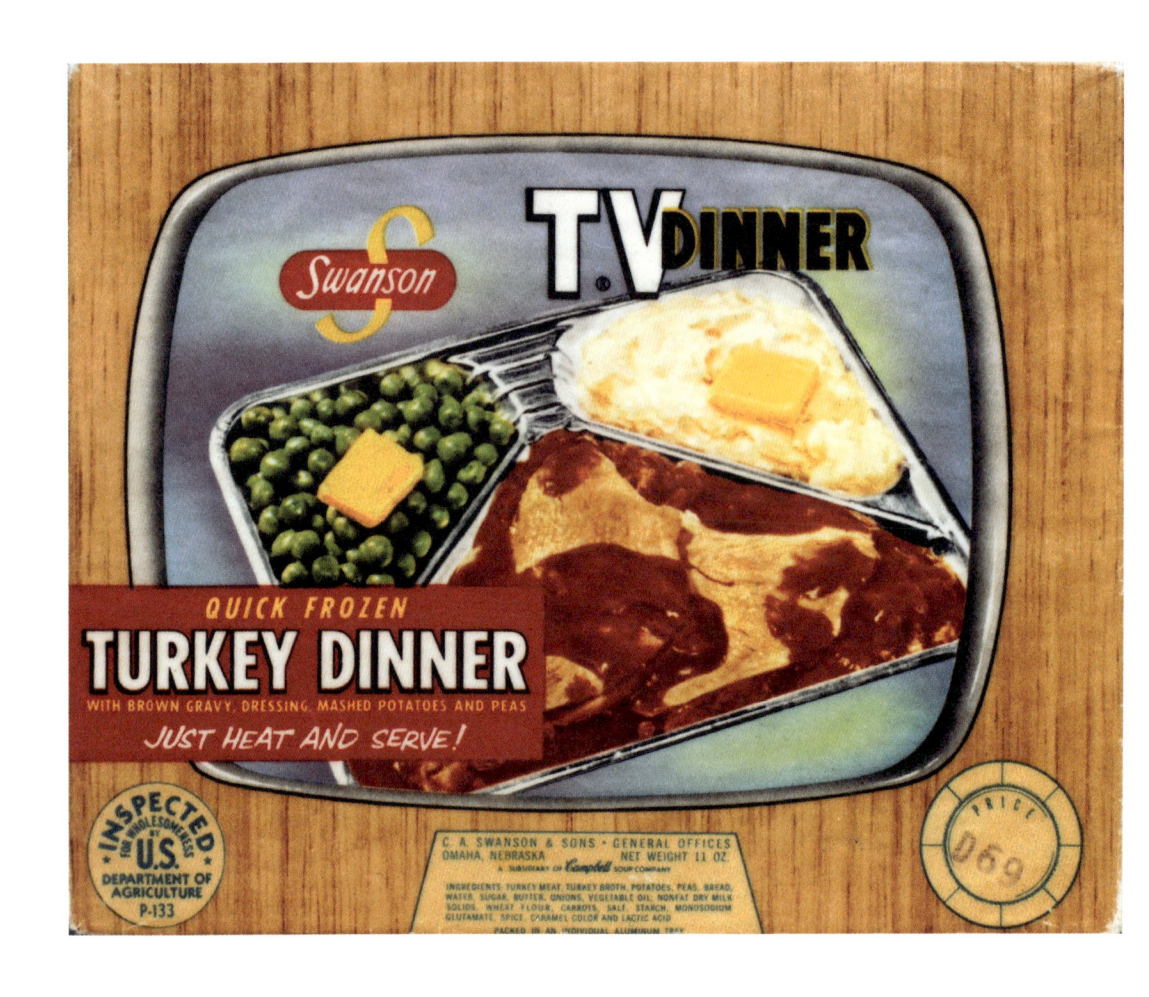

Packaging for Swanson's turkey TV dinner, designed to resemble a television set, 1954

1953

TV DINNERS

TURKEY DINNER WITH BROWN GRAVY

·

MASHED POTATOES

·

GREEN BEANS

THE ADVENT OF TELEVISION as a national pastime in the US – and the rise of more affluent, double-income households – created a perfect storm for the invention of the 'TV' dinner, or 'ready meal', as it came to be known in the UK.

Somewhat humorously, the first TV dinner was one that is usually associated with feasting around a table – Thanksgiving. So the story goes, in 1953, American food company Swanson & Sons were trying to think of ways to use surplus turkey when an employee stumbled across the food trays that airlines were trialling to serve hot meals on board long flights. And so a dinner of turkey, gravy, green beans, mashed potatoes and cranberry sauce was created, complete with packaging that resembled a television screen, including a 'volume' dial. Heralded as the ultimate convenience, TV dinners were seen as a way for working mothers to provide a family meal without having to spend hours at the stove, one of the first taglines for the product being, 'I'm late – but dinner won't be'.

Perhaps surprisingly, it took a good 20 years or so for the trend to cross the pond, although this has to do with freezers being a late-arriving luxury. Britain's love affair has been with the 'ready meal' – chilled, not frozen – and began with a chicken Kiev sold by Marks & Spencer in 1979, followed by Chinese and Indian ready meals in 1985.

'Chikin Ramen' brand instant noodles

1958

NOODLES IN AN INSTANT

INSTANT NOODLES ARE THE fodder of corner shops and supermarkets around the globe, and their entrance into the world of convenience food has been no less seismic than TV dinners in the US and pre-made packaged sandwiches in the UK. The creation of Japanese–Taiwanese inventor Momofuku Ando, the first flash-fried, dried noodles were sold in a single-portion block with chicken flavouring provided in a separate sachet by Ando's company, Nissin, and branded as 'Chikin Ramen'. A more costly product than the fresh noodles sold in shops at the time, dried noodles were at first a luxury, but soon overtook their predecessors to become the most popular choice. In the 1970s, the cup noodle – a plastic container filled with dried noodles and scattered with seasoning – arrived, and now about 100 billion portions of instant noodles are consumed each year around the world. Unlike other convenience foods, technological developments over the years haven't changed the nature of the product; it still takes less than five minutes to cook.

According to a poll conducted in the country, the Japanese rank the invention of instant noodles as one of the country's greatest achievements of the twenty-first century.

The weekday lunchtime staple

1980

SUPERMARKET SANDWICHES

EGG AND CRESS
·
SALMON AND TOMATO
·
PRAWN MAYONNAISE

THE PRE-MADE, PACKAGED SANDWICH is one of those innovations in food that has been revolutionary for both the right and wrong reasons. According to recent market research, the average person living in the UK consumes a routine 20 sandwiches per month, but until 1980, sandwiches were the realm of the home kitchen, the pub or a café, not supermarkets, railway stations or chemists. First trialled by Marks & Spencer in 1980 in five branches across the UK, the offerings on the menu were pretty basic compared to the decidedly lavish fillings available today: egg and cress, salmon and tomato, and prawn mayonnaise. Interestingly, although times have changed, some things do remain constant: these sandwiches are still available at M&S today, and its bestselling is still prawn mayo.

The evolution of the sandwich from scrappy home snack to weekday lunchtime staple is undoubtedly a result of more pressurised working environments – as sandwich counters opened in department stores, cafés in the same buildings began to close. In 1985, Boots became the first company to standardise and nationalise its packaged sandwich distribution, and with it, hot canteen-style lunches soon became a thing of the past.

A Victorian penny ice vendor sells ice cream to an eager crowd

1932

A HISTORY OF ICE CREAM IN THE UK

VANILLA

·

TUTTI FRUTTI

·

CHOCOLATE CHIP

·

RUM AND RAISIN

ICE CREAM, IN ITS VARIOUS guises, has been a popular treat the world over for hundreds of years. It is purportedly a thousand-year-old Chinese invention brought back to Italy in the thirteenth century by Marco Polo. Due to a lack of effective refrigeration, it didn't gain widespread popularity in the UK until the late 1800s. Prior to that, ice harvesting was a big business, and eating a bowl of ice cream a preserve of the European elite. Wall's, the British brand renowned for ice cream (and funnily enough, sausages), were not the first sellers of ice cream by tricycle, despite their slogan 'Stop Me and Buy One' becoming somewhat of a British advertising classic. That practice can be traced back to at least 1907, when Giuseppe Morelli, who had moved from southern Italy to Scotland, began peddling the stuff around the local neighbourhood with his young son. In 1932, the gelato entrepreneur relocated to the well-heeled seaside town of Broadstairs in Kent, thus creating what is now one of the oldest ice-cream parlours in the UK, complete with soda fountain, juke box, leather banquettes, and eight ice-cream flavours, plus a knickerbocker glory – the preserve of British seaside visitors. Popular flavours at the time included vanilla, tutti frutti, chocolate chip, and the somewhat divisive rum and raisin.

DELMONICO'S
FOUNDED 1827

Blue Point oysters 30 Cocktail 35   Cherrystone clams 35 Cocktail 40
Cotuits 35   Cocktail 40   Little Neck clams 30 Cocktail 35
Buzzard Bays 35   Cocktail 40

HORS D'ŒUVRES
Sardines 50   Anchovies 50   Smoked salmon 50   Queen olives 30   Ripe olives 35
Stuffed olives 35   Crab flake cocktail 65   Garden celery 30   Lobster cocktail 80

SOUPS
Purée of lentils 40
Cup, Hanan 60   Purée split pea 40   Oyster stew 55   Green turtle 60 (15 minutes)
Clam broth 35   Tomato 40   Chicken okra 45   Mongol 40   Julienne 40
COLD IN CUP: Consommé 35   Strained gumbo 45   Chicken broth 40

Ready   **EGGS**   *To Order*
Poached, Benedict 45   Shirred à la Turque (2) 65

Ready   **FISH**   *To Order*
Live cod, Dutch style 75   Bluefish, Meunière 75
Fried smelts, Remoulade sauce 75   Striped bass, Maitre d'Hôtel 70
Stuffed crabs 65   Scallops and shrimps, Marinière 80

Plats du Jour   Entrees
Ready   *To Order*
Boiled fowl and rice, celery sauce 1 00   Lamb chop, Robinson 75
Leg of lamb, parsnips in cream 85   Veal kidney saute, Robert 90
Wiener schnitzel, noodles 80   Half Guinea chicken broiled, bacon 1 50
Baked pork and beans 75   Fresh mushrooms on toast 80

ROASTS   GRILL
Ready
Lamb 80   Ribs of beef 90   Chicken (half) 1 30 (whole) 2 50
                              Lamb chops 95   Mutton chop 75

VEGETABLES
Noodles 30   Brussels sprouts 40
Oyster Bay asparagus 65   New string beans 45   Cauliflower in cream 45   French peas 50
Spinach 40   Macaroni 35   Spaghetti 35   New beets in butter 35   Fried egg-plant 30
POTATOES: Boiled new 25   Baked (1) 20   Mashed 25   Sautées 30   Fried 25
Hashed in cream 30   Seybel or Julienne 30   Lyonnaise 35
Hashed in cream, gratinées 35   Sweet potato 25   Hashed browned 30

COLD BUFFET
Lobster, Mayonnaise (half) 1 00   Lobster salad 1 25   Virginia ham 80
Chicken salad 1 00   Crabmeat salad 75   Shrimp salad 75   Beef salad 65
Sliced chicken 90   Smoked ham 65   Lamb 80   Roastbeef 90   Corned beef 65
Beef tongue 75   Assorted meats 1 00   and chicken 1 25

SALADS
Tomato and green pepper 45   Watercress 30   Potato 30   Chiffonade 50   Cucumber 35
Macédoine 50   Beets 35   String beans 45   Lettuce 35   Tomato 35   Romaine 35
Mayonnaise dressing 10 cents extra.

DESSERT
Compot of fresh fruit 45   Plain rice pudding 30   Apple sauce 20   Stewed prunes 30
Vanilla, coffee or chocolate éclairs 20   Rum cake 25   Pie 20
Caramel custard 30   Charlotte Russe 30   Bar-le-Duc jelly 40
Baked apple 20 with cream 30   Fresh fruit tart 25   Cup custard, vanilla or chocolate 25
FRUITS.   Grape fruit, (half) 35   Pineapple 25   Orange 20
         Pear 20   Banana 15   Apple 20
FRENCH ICE CREAMS: Coffee 35   Vanilla 35   Chocolate 35
CHEESE: Gruyère 30 Port-du-Salut 30 Roquefort 50 Gervais 25 American 25 Liederkranz 30
Coffee with milk, pot p. p. 25 for two 35   Tea, pot, p. p. 25 for two 35
    "   "   cream "   35   "   45   Kaffee Hag, demie tasse 20
Kaffee Hag, pot, with cream 40
Horlick's malted milk 10

Beaver & South William Streets.   Tuesday, October 23, 1917

A menu from the iconic New York restaurant Delmonico's

ICONIC MENUS

Where some lead, the rest will follow — and this is particularly true when it comes to groundbreaking food trends. The following pages are odes to the menus of iconic eateries, trailblazers and cultural institutions, from fine dining extravagance to ethically conscious eating.

1893	Delmonico's Trend-Setting Menu
1900	Escoffier at The Ritz
1901	Dinner at New York's Most Famous Hotel
1905	Dinner and Dancing at the Blackpool Tower Ballroom
1937	What to Eat When Crossing the Atlantic
1961	Cranks Vegetarian Restaurant
2014	Neurogastronomy at The Fat Duck

1893

DELMONICO'S TREND-SETTING MENU

CHARLES RANHOFER WAS ALMOST prodigal in his culinary expertise. Sent to Paris at the age of 12 to study pastry, he returned to New York and in 1862, at the age of 26, began to cook at Delmonico's, a restaurant that has become somewhat of an institution over the centuries. As one of the country's most extravagant restaurants, it was supposedly the birthplace of several dishes that have now become part of the canon of classic American cuisine – think baked Alaska, Lobster Newberg, wedge salads, and, during Ranhofer's time, thick-cut steaks, commonly referred to as a Delmonico-style steak. However, many of the back stories of these dishes now sound more mythical than factual: a case in point is Lobster Newberg. The story goes that a famous sea captain, Ben Wenberg, introduced the dish to the restaurant's

Exterior of Delmonico's, New York, date unknown

owner, Lorenzo Delmonico. Upon tasting it, Delmonico insisted that the dish be put on the menu. With a few flourishes and refinements from Ranhofer, the dish appeared, and was an instant hit. But why Newberg? Originally, it was named after the sea captain, but after a dispute, the title changed to an anagram of the captain's name. So popular was Lobster Newberg that it even began to appear in French cookbooks and menus – quite the feat.

This menu, from a sheriff's dinner in 1893, exemplified Ranhofer's style: classic French cooking, with all-American ingredients, including the likes of terrapin from Maryland, American beef with Madeira sauce (a regular on Ranhofer's menus), North American canvasback ducks with hominy beans, and to finish, 'fancy ice creams'.

First Panel Sheriff's Jury Annual Dinner

Wednesday, January 18th, 1893

Delmonico's

MENU

Oysters

SOUPS
Bisque of Crabs   Green Turtle, clear

SIDE DISH
Timbales, Reynière

FISH
Fillet of Bass, Joinville
Potatoes, Dauphine

REMOVE
Fillet of Beef with Madeira
Tomatoes, Trevise

ENTRÉES
Breast of Chicken, Genin
Peas, Parisian fashion

Terrapin, Maryland

SHERBET, PRUNELLE

ROAST
Canvas-back Ducks   (Fried Hominy)

COLD
Terrine of foies gras with Jelly
Lettuce Salad

SWEET
Pears, Ferrières

Pyramids

Fancy Ice Creams   Fruits   Cakes
Coffee

Chablis
Sherry

Liebfraumilch
Chât. Lagrange
Champagne

Macon Vieux
Liqueurs
Apollinaris

Menu from Delmonico's, 1893

Title page of Ranhofer's book *The Epicurean*, published in 1894

Dîner du 26 Juin 1900

MENU

Melon

Consommé Rossini

Crème Princesse

Truite Saumonée Norvégienne

Suprêmes de Volaille aux Artichauts

Selle de Pré-Salé à la broche

Petits Pois Française

Pommes nouvelles

Sorbets au Kirsch

Caneton de Rouen Vendôme

Cœurs de Romaine

Asperges Sauce Mousseline

Biscuit glacé Viennois

Friandises

Corbeilles de Fruits

VINS

Xérès	Pommery 1893 sec et doux
Château Caillou 1888	Grand vin
Château Smith Lafitte 1878	Château Giscours 1874

HOTEL RITZ　　　　　　　　　　　　　　　　　　　　PARIS

Menu from The Ritz Paris, 1900

1900

ESCOFFIER AT THE RITZ

AUGUSTE ESCOFFIER IS, UNDOUBTEDLY, one of the most important figures in European culinary history. A disciple of Marie-Antoine Carême's elaborate and extravagant cooking style, Escoffier created a streamlined, elegant version of that approach, which has become what is regarded as the origination of classic French cooking. One of his most famous achievements was *Le Guide Culinaire*, a book that is still widely used for reference to this day, in which he identified five 'mother' sauces as the backbone of French cuisine. In addition to these achievements, Escoffier was chef at some of Europe's most esteemed hotels – The Savoy in London, and latterly, The Ritz in Paris. The chef arrived at the former in 1890 from the south of France, where he had been employed by Caesar Ritz to manage The Grand Hotel in Monte Carlo. During his and Ritz's eight-year tenure at The Savoy – the hotel manager went with him to London – he garnered high-society followers from the Prince of Wales to French actor Sarah Bernhardt.

Escoffier and Caesar Ritz were dismissed from the hotel under suspicion of fraud some five years later, but as a result, the two went on to set up The Ritz in Paris – and so out of misfortune, an institution was created. This menu, from The Ritz, contains so many instantly recognisable dishes that it could almost read as one of a classic French bistro from the twenty-first century: consommé, chicken supreme with artichokes, kirsch sorbet to cleanse the palate, and for dessert, friands and fruits.

Supper

| Malpecques 40 | Cape Cods 30 | Bluepoints 30 | Cotuits 30 |

Bieluga Caviare 1 50   Pim-Olas 35   Lyon Sausage 50
Sardines 35   Carciofini 40   Antipasti 40
Radishes 25   Pickled Lamb's Tongue 40   Anchovies 50

HOT

Chicken Broth per cup 30   Chicken Broth, Bellevue per cup 30
Consommé cup 25   Clam Broth cup 25

Terrapin 3 50   Oyster Crabs 1 00
Stuffed Lobster 60   Crab Meat, Astoria 1 00
Lobster Cutlets, Cream sauce 60   Lobster, Bordelaise 1 25
Stuffed Crab 50   Broiled Lobster 1 00   Devilled Kidneys 50
Bouchée, Capucin 1 00   Chicken à la King 1 50
Canapé Waldorf 60   Sweetbreads, Waldorf 1 25
Boneless Hamburg Chicken 1 50   Lamb Chops, St. Hilaire 85
Scotch Woodcock 50   Welsh Rarebit 40   Yorkshire Buck 60

Broiled Chicken 2 00 half 1 00   Broiled Squab 90   Broiled Sweetbread 1 00
Tournedos of Filet, Cherron 1 50

Partridge 2 50   Mallard Duck 2 00   Woodcock 2 50

French Asparagus 1 25   German Asparagus 1 00
Artichoke, Hollandaise 60   Oyster Bay Asparagus 75

COLD

Partridge 2 50   Plover 90
Game Pie 1 25   Spring Lamb 80   Crabs, Ravigotte 60
Mixed Cold Meat 75   with Chicken 1 00   Fantaisie, Joseph 1 25
Beef à la Mode 75   Boneless Squab in jelly 1 10   Boned Capon 1 00
Westphalian Ham 75   Squab 90   Virginia Ham 75

Sandwiches:—Tongue 25   Chicken 30   Caviare 40
Sardine 30   Paté de foie gras 50   Club 35
Canapé à la Rex 50   Ham 25

Crab 75   Romaine 50   Alexander 75   Russian 1 00   Cucumbers 50
Lettuce 50   Chicken 1 00   Florida 75   Lobster 1 00
Tomato 50   Dixie 60   Japonaise 1 00

Nesselrode Pudding 40   Mixed Cakes 25   Sorbet au Curaçao 30
Café Parfait 25   Chestnut Plombière 40   Biscuit glacé 30
Charlotte Russe 25   Eclairs 25
Caramel Custard 30   Coupe St. Jacques 60

ICES IN SOUVENIRS 75
Peach Ice Cream 25   Peach frappée 25
Vanilla, Strawberry, Pistache, Coffee or Chocolate Ice Cream 25   Mixed 30
Apricot, Raspberry, Lemon, Orange or Pineapple Water Ice 25
French Coffee, Cup 15   Turkish Coffee 20

APOLLINARIS 40 20   **JOHANNIS 40 20**

11. Oct. 1905   10-11-05

Menu from the Waldorf-Astoria, 1905

1897

DINNER AT NEW YORK'S MOST FAMOUS HOTEL

CANAPE DE CAVIARE

·

GRILLED BEEF

·

WALDORF SALAD

THE WALDORF-ASTORIA IN New York's midtown Manhattan is, arguably, the most famous hotel in the world. It was originally two separate hotels: the Waldorf on one side of the road, opening in 1893, and the Astoria, constructed in 1897. Owned by the Astor family, a renowned, high-society family, the first hotel was named after the town in Germany from which they originated, and the inspiration for the name of the second hotel perhaps requires no guesswork.

Upon opening, the concept was much derided; seen as an unnecessary addition to a well-to-do neighbourhood by locals, and far too expensive for those travelling to the city for business, its original purpose was unclear. However, after a succession of fundraising dinners, it became loved by the high-society crowd, and so its reputation was cemented, with the wealthy from around the world flocking to stay in the largest – and most opulent – hotel of the time. The first hotel in the world to offer room service, the Waldorf-Astoria is also responsible for the popularity of a handful of globally recognised dishes: the eponymous Waldorf Salad, made with apples, celery, grapes and walnuts; eggs Benedict (although it's debatable as to whether this was first served here); and Thousand Island dressing. This menu from 1905 epitomises the extravagance with which the hotel is associated: game pie for $1.25 and foie gras for 50 cents, was, at the time, big bucks – and judging by its loyal clientele, for good reason.

THE TOWER

Café Restaurant

The Most Beautiful Dining Room out of London.

EVERYTHING OF THE BEST

AT REASONABLE PRICES.

FOUR BILLIARD TABLES

(By Borroughes & Watts)

ADMISSION FREE

From Promenade and Bank Hey Street.

Advert in the Blackpool Tower programme, July 1905

1905

DINNER AND DANCING AT THE BLACKPOOL TOWER BALLROOM

MUTTON CHOPS

·

RUMP STEAK

·

GROVES AND WHITNALL ALES AND STOUTS

AN ICON OF THE highs and lows of the British seaside, Blackpool is inextricably linked with its 518-foot tower, a replica of Paris's most famous landmark. Today, it's recognised as a masterful example of Victorian architecture, but at the time, it was an innovative addition to the thriving coastal resort, which incorporated an aquarium, a circus complete with exotic animals and resident clowns, a ballroom for variety performances and dances, and a restaurant furnished with a mezzanine level for orchestral performances.

The tower and the red-brick complex beneath took three years to construct from start to finish, and, according to an 1895 brochure for the tower and its attractions, saw up to 50,000 visitors pass through its doors on a bank holiday weekend. The ballroom boasted the country's longest bar, which was decorated with 'splendid mirrors, magnificent faience panelling, and thorough display of all the fittings … altogether one of the finest displays that can be seen anywhere in the kingdom'. The Tower Restaurant was no less elegant, complete with its own 'fountain whose fairy jets upon occasion are electrically illuminated', situated in the centre of the room. The grill, it is said, was exceptionally fine – mutton chops and rump steaks were the order of the day, served with Groves and Whitnall ales and stouts. While the glory bestowed upon the Blackpool Tower and its facilities has faded somewhat, its status as a cultural institution remains.

R.M.S. "QUEEN MARY"　　　　　　　　　Friday, April 23, 1937

Luncheon

Consomme Brunoise　　　　　　　　　Potage St. Germain

Supreme of Whitefish Vin Blanc
Salmon Fish Cakes Maryland

Scrambled Eggs with Truffles
Braised Ox Tail Printaniere
Macaroni al Sugo

Roast Loin of Pork and Dressing, Apple Sauce
Broccoli en Puree　　　　　　　　　Mashed Turnips
Baked Jacket and Fried Potatoes

Grilled Tenderloin Hamburger and Onions

COLD:
Roast Beef, Horseradish Sauce
Galantine of Veal　　　London Brawn　　　Pressed Beef
Roast Lamb, Mint Sauce

Salads—Romaine　　　　　Tomato
Mixed Pickles

Boiled Jam Roll Pudding, Cream Sauce

Ice Cream and Wafers

Cheese　　　　　　　Rolls

Tea　　　　　　　　Coffee

Passengers on Special Diet are invited to make known their requirements to the Chief Third Class Steward

T/C

Menu from RMS *Queen Mary*, 1937

1937

WHAT TO EAT WHEN CROSSING THE ATLANTIC

THE TRANSATLANTIC JOURNEY between Western Europe and New York City is perhaps one of the most romanticised routes of all time. With crossings taking between six and seven days, it's easy to see why a trip like this becomes as much of an event as the destination itself.

RMS *Queen Mary*, one of the short-lived and somewhat doomed vessels created by the Cunard-White Star Line, was one of the most elaborately decorated liners of the 1930s, and sailed from Southampton to Cherbourg and on to New York. In keeping with the art deco style of the time, she was sleek and elegant, and garnered the nickname 'Ship of Woods', as there were reportedly 50 different kinds of wood used in furnishings and adornments. First-class passengers included everyone from Winston Churchill and T. S. Eliot to Elizabeth Taylor and Walt Disney; while this menu might sound like it was fit for a movie star, it was actually set for third-class passengers, and typical of a daily lunch on board. The food reflects tastes from every port on the journey, including Maryland-style crab cakes, hamburgers, braised oxtail printanière, and the very British roast beef with horseradish sauce.

Across the classes, the dining rooms, and the food served, were elaborate affairs, but the ship's finery was short-lived, as it was turned into transportation for troops in the Second World War before being returned to commercial use. Her final voyage was on 31 October 1967, where she set sail for the west coast of America, to a permanent mooring in Long Beach, California. The liner now serves as a tourist attraction, complete with museum, bars, restaurants and entertainment.

Illustration of the front cover of the lunch menu

Illustration from the original Cranks cookbook

1961

CRANKS VEGETARIAN RESTAURANT

HOMITY PIE

·

LENTIL SALAD

·

CHEESE SCONES

WHILE ETHICAL VEGETARIANISM and a belief in whole foods for healthy living certainly existed before the 1960s, it wasn't until this revolutionary decade that plant-based eating became more widely part of the mainstream consciousness. There were, indeed, vegetarian restaurants as far back as the Victorian period – for example, the Pitman Vegetarian Hotel in Birmingham opened in 1898, named after the Vegetarian Society's vice president of the time, and was running well into the 1930s. But David Canter, founder of Cranks, took a chance on opening a whole-foods salad bar in London's vibrant Carnaby Street, and was swept up by the free-spirited zeitgeist that was gaining momentum by 1961. The restaurant served wholemeal bread, cakes and savoury pastries, along with a self-serve salad and cheese buffet from which customers were encouraged to eat as much as they liked. Homity pie, lentil salads and cheese scones were often the order of the day, and what the restaurant became known for – but as the menu was dependent on the available produce, it changed almost daily. Soon, Cranks gained a fashionable following. Recommended in *Tatler* in 1961, with a special nod to the 'unusual decor' – wooden tables, handmade ceramics, mismatched soft furnishings – it developed a celebrity fanbase, including the likes of Paul and Linda McCartney and Princess Diana. That one salad bar turned into a chain of restaurants over the decades, with the last branch sadly closing in 2016.

NITRO POACHED APERITIFS

Vodka and Lime Sour, Gin and Tonic, Tequila and Grapefruit

RED CABBAGE GAZPACHO

Pommery Grain Mustard Ice Cream

JELLY OF QUAIL, CRAYFISH CREAM

Chicken Liver Parfait, Oak Moss and Truffle Toast

(Homage to Alain Chapel)

SNAIL PORRIDGE

Iberico Bellota Ham, Shaved Fennel

SCALLOP IN AMOND MILK

ROAST FOIE GRAS

Barberry, Confit Kombu and Crab Biscuit

MAD HATTER'S TEA PARTY

(c. 1892)

Mock Turtle Soup, Pocket Watch and Toast Sandwich

A 2014 menu from The Fat Duck

1995

NEUROGASTRONOMY AT THE FAT DUCK

RARELY IN THE HISTORY of the UK has a restaurant, or indeed a chef, been as talked about as The Fat Duck and its chef, Heston Blumenthal. Based on the site of a traditional old pub in the village of Bray in Hampshire, the restaurant opened in 1995. Since then, it's gained three Michelin stars and held the title of World's Best Restaurant. Although it started out serving (believe it or not) steak and chips, The Fat Duck became synonymous with what's known as multi-sensory cooking – a technique that incorporates senses such as sound into the dining experience, as demonstrated by one of the restaurant's most iconic dishes, Sound of the Sea. As diners ate a variety of shellfish and edible seaweed, they listened to the waves crashing against rocks on a beach. While neurogastronomy may not be something that's a priority of the masses, Blumenthal's explorations into a way of immersive eating that's almost an art form have garnered interest – and praise – from around the world. As the chef himself says, food 'has the ability to generate so much memory and emotion'. Also on the menu were the controversial snail porridge, and bacon and egg ice cream – revolutionary, subjective and subversive in equal measure.

MAINS

MENUS DON'T JUST REFLECT popular food trends. They can form part of a broader picture of social and historical context, and tell a story not just about a particular situation, but the legacy that was subsequently created. This chapter is all about 'main' events — menus that, in their conception, or simply by their occurrence, encapsulate social and political change, from Queen Victoria's Diamond Jubilee in 1897 and the first-ever Nobel Prize dinner in 1901, to the Red Cross' First World War canteen offerings and hospital food served by the newly formed NHS in 1948. But while these menus reflect wider cultural context, others threw light on changes taking place within households, too — those found in cookbooks. A menu from *Mrs Beeton's Book of Household Management*, for example, speaks volumes about Victorian social mobility, while Marguerite Patten's first cookbook in colour set a precedent for the glossy tomes of today.

Front cover of the Christmas edition of *Blighty* magazine

MEALS THAT MADE HISTORY

Breaking bread often goes hand in hand with significant events. Whether presented at congregations of world leaders, presidential inaugaurations or celebrations of political progress, these menus had one thing in common — food that reflected past, present and future.

1897   Queen Victoria's Diamond Jubilee Luncheon

1901   First Nobel Prize Dinner

1917   Christmas in the Trenches

1918   Suffragettes' Victory Dinner

1943   Stalin, Churchill and Roosevelt at the Tehran Conference

1943   UN Peace Dinner

1947   Indian Independence Dinner

1959   Khrushchev's California Railway Dinner

1961   JFK's Inauguration Lunch

2009   Barack Obama's First Meal in the White House

Buckingham Palace.
JUNE 21st, 1897.
HER MAJESTY'S DINNER.

Queen's Table.
- The Queen
- The Prince of Naples
- Princess of Wales
- Grand Duke of Hesse
- Prince Albert of Prussia
- Grand Duchess Elizabeth Feodorovna of Russia
- Grand Duke of Mecklenburg-Strelitz
- Grand Duke Serge of Russia
- Grand Duchess of Hesse
- Crown Prince of Siam
- Empress Frederick
- The Archduke Francis Ferdinand of Austria

Prince of Wales's Table.
- Prince of Wales
- Princess Christian of Schleswig-Holstein
- Grand Duke of Mecklenburg-Strelitz
- Princess Frederica of Hanover
- The Prince of Japan
- Princess of Bulgaria
- Prince Henry of Prussia
- Duc d'Aumale (France), Special Ambassador
- Princess Henry of Prussia
- Prince Waldemar of Denmark
- Duchess of Saxe-Coburg and Gotha
- Prince Henry of Prussia
- The Princess of Naples

Duke of Saxe-Coburg and Gotha's Table.
- Duke of Saxe-Coburg and Gotha
- Duchess of Connaught
- Prince Rupert of Bavaria
- Duchess of York
- Duke of Oporto
- Princess Victoria of Wales
- The Hon. Whitelaw Reid, United States Special Ambassador
- Hereditary Princess of Saxe-Meiningen
- Prince Frederick Augustus, Duke of Saxony
- Princess Louise (Duchess of Fife)
- Grand Duke Cyril of Russia
- Princess Louise (Marchioness of Lorne)

Duke of Connaught's Table.
- Duke of Connaught
- Princess Beatrice, Princess Henry of Battenberg
- Duchess of Albany
- Duke Albert of Wurtemberg
- Princess Charles of Denmark
- Crown Prince of Montenegro
- Prince Charles de Ligne, Belgian Minister Extraordinary
- Duke of Sotomayor, Spanish Special Ambassador
- Monsignor Sambucetti, Archbishop of Corinth, Papal Envoy
- Hereditary Grand Duke of Luxemburg
- Princess Adolphe of Schaumburg-Lippe
- Prince Eugene of Sweden and Norway

Duke of York's Table.
- Duke of York
- Princess Frederick Charles of Hesse
- Prince of Bulgaria
- Princess Louis of Battenberg
- Prince Alfred of Saxe-Coburg
- M. de Staal (Russian Ambassador)
- His Excellency Chang Ying Hun (China)
- Prince Mohammed Ali, Pacha of Egypt
- Prince Amir Khan of Persia
- Princess Victoria of Schleswig-Holstein
- Prince Charles of Denmark
- Duchess of Teck

Duke of Cambridge's Table.
- Duke of Cambridge
- Princess Feodore of Saxe-Meiningen
- Prince Philip of Saxe-Coburg
- Prince Edward of Saxe-Weimar
- Duke of Teck
- Munir Pacha (Turkish Envoy)
- Count van Lynden
- Duchess of Buccleuch (Mistress of the Robes)
- Princess Hatzfeldt, Mistress of the Robes (to The Empress Frederick)
- Prince Frederick Charles of Hesse
- Prince Aribert of Anhalt
- Princess Aribert of Anhalt

Marquis of Lorne's Table.
- Marquis of Lorne
- Count de Casa Valencia (Spanish Ambassador)
- Prince Adolphus of Teck
- Prince Francis of Teck
- Baron von Hammingen
- Pawel Hammingen
- Anthopoulo Pacha (Turkish Ambassador)
- Prince Alexander of Teck
- Min Young hwan (Corean Envoy)
- Lord Chamberlain
- Duke of Fife
- Prince Albert of Schleswig-Holstein
- Countess Victoria Gleichen

Prince Christian of Schleswig-Holstein's Table.
- Prince Christian of Schleswig-Holstein
- Countess Feodora Gleichen
- Prince Hermann of Saxe-Weimar
- Count Deym (Austro-Hungarian Ambassador)
- Prince Louis of Battenberg
- Herr von Bauer
- M. de Courcel (French Ambassador)
- The Marquis of Salisbury
- Mr. Hay, United States Ambassador
- General Ferrero (Italian Ambassador)
- The Archbishop of Finland
- The Lord Steward
- Prince Christian Victor of Schleswig-Holstein
- Count Hatzfeldt (German Ambassador)
- Princess Adolphe of Schaumburg-Lippe
- Princess Victor of Hohenlohe

The table configuration and settings at the Diamond Jubilee celebrations

1897

QUEEN VICTORIA'S DIAMOND JUBILEE LUNCHEON

QUEEN VICTORIA'S DIAMOND JUBILEE held dual significance – before Queen Elizabeth II surpassed the length of her reign in 2015, this was the longest of any monarch in British history. The event was declared a festival of the British Empire, involving all the territories of the UK – at this point, Victoria was monarch of some 450 million people. Although the Queen's popularity had dipped in the years following the death of her husband, at this time there was an economic boom as a result of industrialisation and expansion, and Victoria's popularity surged. Jubilee Day was 22 June, with several public appearances and a procession through the city of London alongside leaders of self-governing British dominions and the Indian states. At an official dinner on the eve of the processions, 21 June, a feast with a decidedly French accent was served to family and dignitaries. A meal of multiple courses was served, plus a buffet, where guests ate the likes of Scotch broth, chicken with rice and English-style peas. The additional buffet items included a rather vaguely described dish of 'hot and cold roast fowls', and tomato salad.

Overleaf: The menus from both the household and the royal celebrations

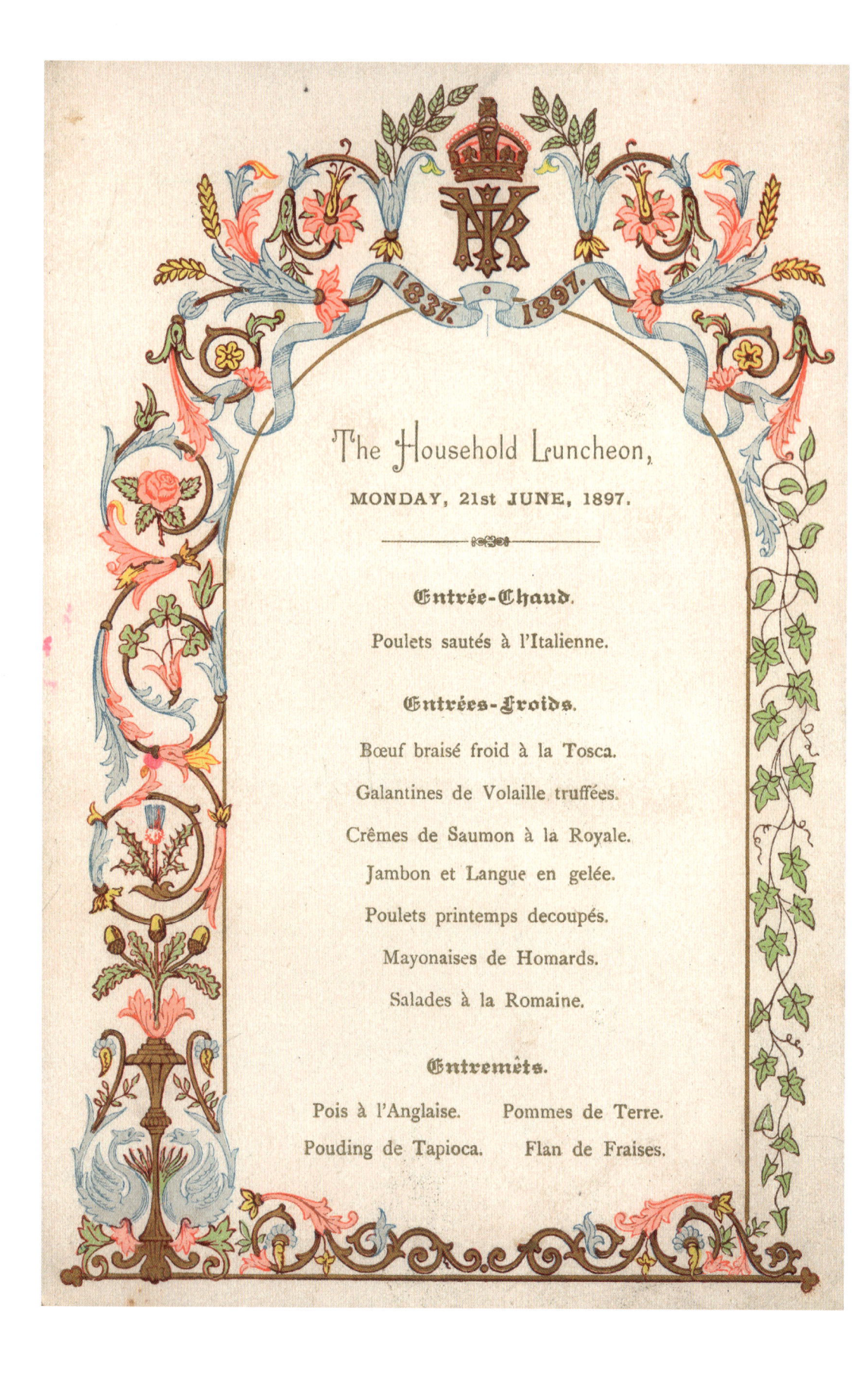

The Household Luncheon,

MONDAY, 21st JUNE, 1897.

Entrée-Chaud.

Poulets sautés à l'Italienne.

Entrées-Froids.

Bœuf braisé froid à la Tosca.

Galantines de Volaille truffées.

Crêmes de Saumon à la Royale.

Jambon et Langue en gelée.

Poulets printemps decoupés.

Mayonaises de Homards.

Salades à la Romaine.

Entremêts.

| Pois à l'Anglaise. | Pommes de Terre. |
| Pouding de Tapioca. | Flan de Fraises. |

The Royal Luncheon,

Monday. 21st June, 1897.

Potage.
Brunoise.

Entrées-Chauds.
Filets de Bœuf à la Milanaise.
Selles d'Agneau rôties.
Kalbs Côteletten mit Krauterne.

Entrées-Froids.
Poulets en gelée à la Renaissance
Crêmes de Saumon à la Royale.
Salades à la Parisienne.

Entremêts.
Pois à l'Anglaise.   Pommes de terre.
Pouding de Tapioca.   Flans de Fraises.

BUFFET.
Hot and Cold Roast Fowls.   Tongue.
Cold Beef.   Galantines.

The first Nobel Prize laureates (clockwise from top left): Henry Dunant, Wilhelm Conrad Röntgen, Frédéric Passy, Sully Prudhomme, Emil von Behring, Jacobus H. van 't Hoff

1901

FIRST NOBEL PRIZE DINNER

HORS D'ŒUVRE

·

SUPREME OF BRILL, NORMANDY STYLE

·

FILLET OF BEEF

·

ROASTED HAZEL GROUSE

·

SUCCÈS GRAND HÔTEL PÂTISSERIE

WHILE THE NOBEL PRIZE is much lauded today, its origins are a little more complex. Conceived by inventor Alfred Nobel – whose most famous creation was dynamite – the prize was a result of the last of his many wills. Eight years before his death in 1896, an obituary was published in a French newspaper, mistakenly thinking that Alfred had passed, when in fact it was his brother, engineer Ludvig Nobel. Preoccupied by how his legacy would be viewed, Alfred decided to act, and left his considerable fortune to a foundation that would award financial prizes to those deemed to confer the 'greatest benefit to mankind' each year. The first ceremony was held on 10 December 1901, five years to the day of his death. Four prizes – those for Physics, Chemistry, Medicine and Literature – were awarded at the Royal Swedish Academy of Music in Stockholm, while the Peace prize – arguably the most talked-about recognition in modern times – was held in Oslo, then known as Christiana, in Norway. The winners included Wilhelm Conrad Röntgen in Physics, due to his discovery of X-rays; Jacobus H. van 't Hoff in Chemistry for his work on osmotic pressure in animal and plant life; Emil von Behring in Medicine, whose work focused on finding a cure for diptheria; Sully Prudhomme for Literature; and Henry Dunant, founder of the International Committee of the Red Cross, who shared the Peace prize with Frédéric Passy, an internationally regarded pacifist. After the ceremony, guests were invited to The Grand Hotel for a celebratory dinner. A classically French menu was served, including brill in a butter sauce, fillet of beef, and hazel grouse (known in French as *gelinottes*), which was a delicacy at the turn of the century. For dessert, high-end pâtisserie was brought all the way from the Succès Grand Hôtel in Bordeaux, France, and served with sweet sherry.

XMAS 1917 BELGIUM

MENU

8 O'CLOCK. BREAKFAST. BACON. LIVER. TOMATOES. COFFEE.

12.30 PM. LUNCH. COLD MEAT. BREAD. PICKLES. SAUCE. BEER. STOUT. COFFEE.

4.30 PM. DINNER. 4.30 PM.

ROAST PORK — APPLE SAUCE.
PEAS. POTATOES. ONIONS.
PLUM PUDDING & CUSTARD.
APPLES. ORANGES. DATES.
COFFEE & BISCUITS. NUTS & WINE.
SWEETS. BEER & STOUT.
TOBACCO. CIGARS. CIGARETTES.

WITH APOLOGIES TO VON TIRPITZ AND THE 'U' BOAT MENACE!

BY KIND PERMISSION OF THE BOYS HOLDING THE LINE!

A handwritten menu from Christmas Day in the trenches, 1917

1917

CHRISTMAS IN THE TRENCHES

MUCH HAS BEEN WRITTEN about the Christmas truce of 1914, when troops in the trenches unofficially held a ceasefire, singing carols, exchanging rations, tobacco and drinks, and even playing football. While this event was sadly a one-off, efforts continued to be made back in Britain to bring a little festive spirit to the men and women serving in the First World War. Each year, parcels of sweets and tobacco were sent to Indian and British troops. In 1914, the Army Commander-in-Chief's wife organised a drive for women to knit scarves for those on the front – it was reported that 250,000 items were sent.

This menu, from 1917, was served to the Army Ordnance Corps in Belgium. Soldiers behind the front line were afforded the relative luxury of some semblance of a Christmas meal, while those on the front line, sadly, would still have received the usual rations, with a few extra treats thrown in where possible. This feast of roast pork with apple sauce, plum pudding, fruits, nuts, sweets and cigarettes was a far cry from the everyday meals of all soldiers in 1917. No matter where they were stationed, troops normally sat down to Maconchie's meat stew – which contained fattier and therefore cheaper cuts of beef – with potatoes, carrots and onions, and hard biscuits.

Illustration entitled 'Melody and Merriment Ringing in the Trenches' from *The War Illustrated*, 1917

An illustration of the Christmas truce of 1917 in *Illustrated London News*

"Victory" Dinner,

FEBRUARY 22ND, 1918.

MENU.

Consommé Julienne.
ou
Crême de Volaille.

Turbot à la Mornay.
Pommes Nouvellee.

Lentil Cutlets and Tomato Sauce.
Eggs à l'Italienne.

Tarte de Rhubarbe.
Crême à la Vanilla.

Café.

The Suffragettes' 'Victory Dinner' menu, 1918

1918

SUFFRAGETTES' VICTORY DINNER

UPON OPENING ITS DOORS in 1916, the Minerva Café in London's Holborn acted as a meeting space and vegetarian café for various factions of the suffragette, communist and anarchist movements. The café was also the headquarters of the Women's Freedom League; in *The Vote*, a suffragette newspaper circulated at the time, the café was described as 'the best and most attractive place in or near the city and West End for well-cooked, daintily served meals'. On a separate note, it was stated that 'the managers will be grateful to friends who will help them by sending comfortable chairs, a Chesterfield couch, and a piano.' Vegetarianism was very common within the movement, and many also campaigned against wearing fur, eating meat and animal testing. The February 1918 dinner was hosted by the WFL in celebration of the passing of The Representation of the People Act, which allowed some women to vote. The WFL served a 'Victory Dinner' that was pescatarian: turbot with mornay sauce, lentil cutlets, and rhubarb tart. At the Minerva, even the crockery reflected the message of the activists who ran it: 'dare to be free'. Eventually evolving into the Minerva Club, an establishment open to men and women with radical political leanings, it finally closed its doors in 1959, but a plaque dedicated to the women who first established it remains.

Stalin, Roosevelt and Churchill at the Tehran conference, 1943

1943

STALIN, CHURCHILL AND ROOSEVELT AT THE TEHRAN CONFERENCE

PERSIAN BARLEY SOUP

POACHED TROUT WITH BELUGA CAVIAR

ROAST TURKEY WITH ROAST POTATOES AND SEASONAL VEGETABLES

SAFFRON ICE CREAM

CHEESE SOUFFLÉ

THE MEETING OF ALLIED LEADERS in Iran's capital signified a shift in perspective on the Second World War. Winston Churchill, Franklin D. Roosevelt and Joseph Stalin, in the same room together for the first time, agreed to unite on a second front to further discuss their intention to defeat Nazi Germany, and to form a 'United Nations' to 'banish the scourge and terror of war for many generations'. Talks as part of a four-day conference held at the Soviet Embassy were inevitably intense. The third day, however, was Winston Churchill's birthday, and it was decided that the British prime minister would host a dinner at the British Embassy to celebrate the event. For his 69th birthday dinner on 30 November, Churchill's chosen menu was classically British, with a couple of Middle Eastern flourishes as a nod to the location: Bloody Mary cocktails to start; Persian barley soup; poached trout with caviar; roast turkey; saffron ice cream, and finally, a cheese soufflé. The pièce de résistance was the birthday cake, adorned with 69 candles in shape of the letter 'V' for 'victory', which the prime minister blew out with Stalin seated on one side, and Roosevelt on the other.

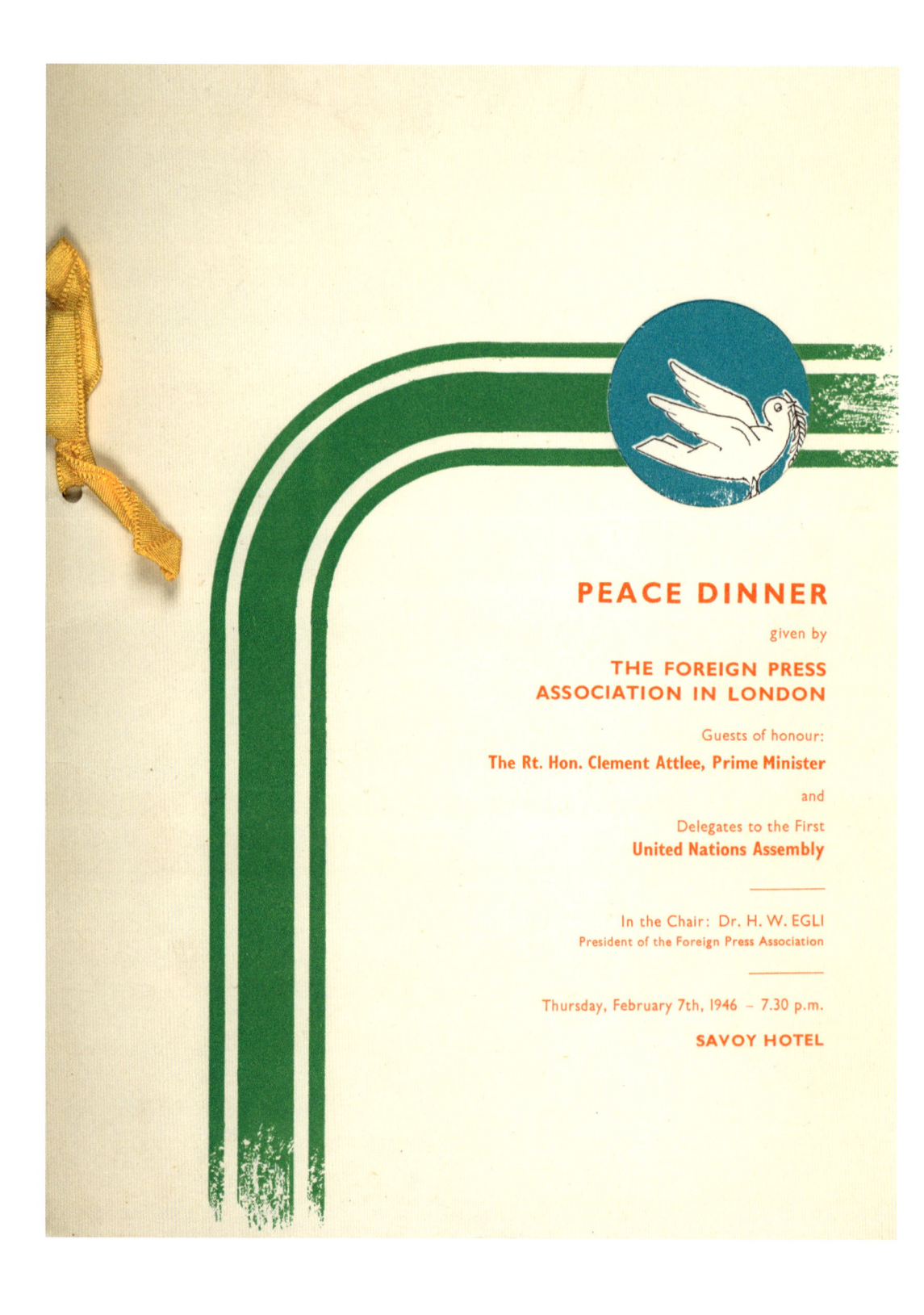

PEACE DINNER

given by

THE FOREIGN PRESS ASSOCIATION IN LONDON

Guests of honour:

The Rt. Hon. Clement Attlee, Prime Minister

and

Delegates to the First
United Nations Assembly

In the Chair: Dr. H. W. EGLI
President of the Foreign Press Association

Thursday, February 7th, 1946 – 7.30 p.m.

SAVOY HOTEL

Cover for the Foreign Press Association's UN Peace Dinner, 1946

1946

UN PEACE DINNER

OFFICIALLY COMING INTO EXISTENCE in 1945, the United Nations – at first a collective of 51 countries – gathered in San Francisco, California, to draw up a charter that was to be the blueprint for the maintenance of international peace. Driven by an urge to prevent further global unrest following the disastrous ramifications of the Second World War, the so-called Allied Big Four – the United States of America, the United Kingdom, the Soviet Union and China – held negotiations from as early as October 1944 to agree on the obligations and conditions of this newly established international governmental organisation. The details, history and legacy of this are highly nuanced in a way that would be impossible to describe in a few short sentences, but suffice to say, the first UN General Assembly took place in London, on 17 January 1946. An event hosted by the Foreign Press Association in London – itself a politically non-aligned organisation – followed three weeks after. With the British prime minister, Clement Atlee, as guest of honour, UN delegates and FPA associates gathered for the so-called Peace Dinner at The Savoy hotel. The playful 'menu', complete with cariactures of world leaders, a salmon in a bowler hat and a winged Uncle Sam, gave satirical nods to member states and political preoccupations – think plat de resistance, bombe glacée atomique and chinoiseries Russo-Persanes. How this translated on a plate is undocumented, but one thing to be sure of is that it was served with a sense of humour.

Saumon Canadien en boîte *

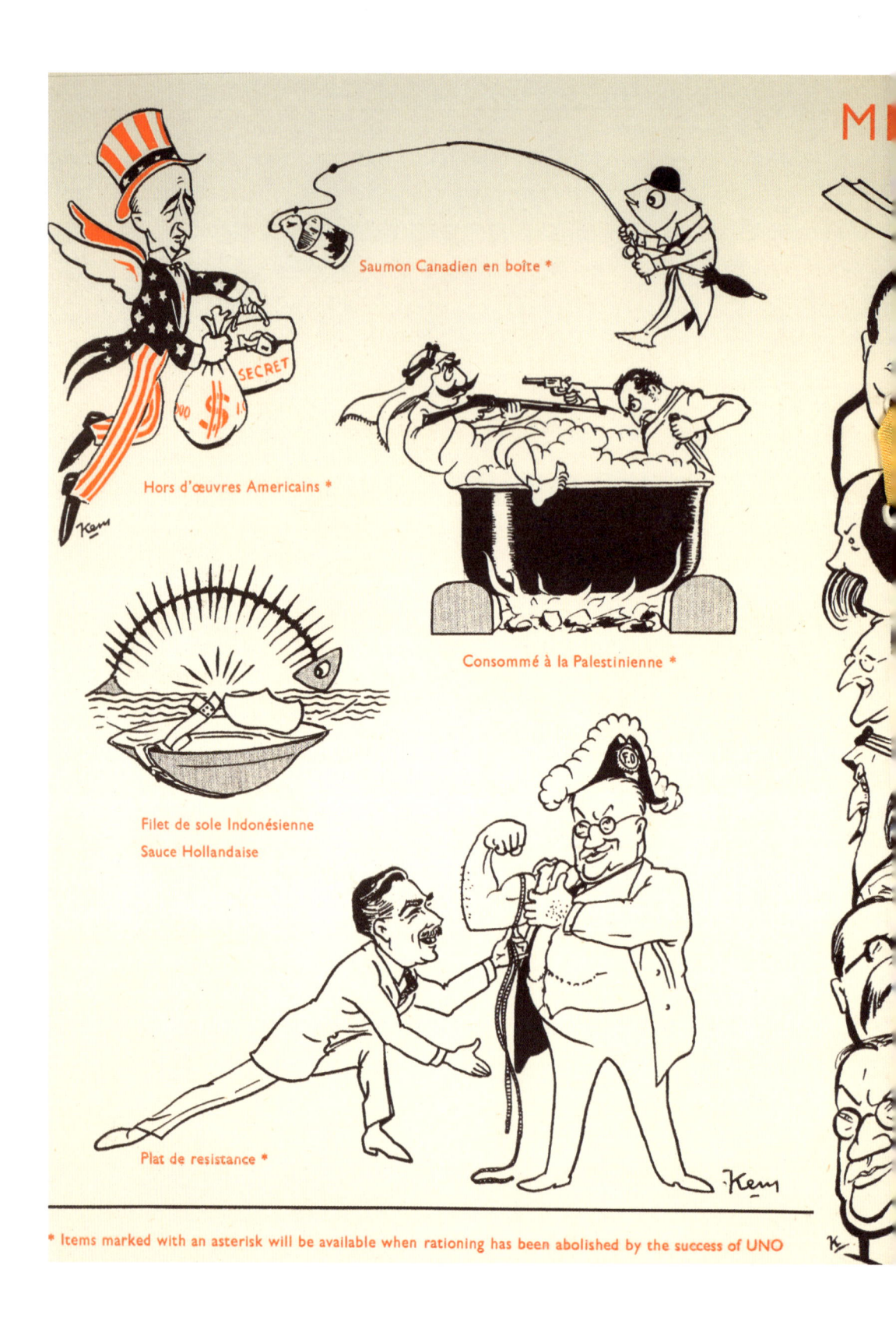

Hors d'œuvres Americains *

Consommé à la Palestinienne *

Filet de sole Indonésienne
Sauce Hollandaise

Plat de resistance *

* Items marked with an asterisk will be available when rationing has been abolished by the success of UNO

The FPA's quirky, illustrated take on the evening's menu

Pintade Internationale à la façon des Grands Trois. Petits pois. Grandes espérances

Bombe glacée Atomique

Chinoiseries Russo-Persanes

Café du Brésil

Savoury: Coxcomb on horseback *

VINS

Cocktails, "Molotoff" etc.

Grand Vin Soi-disant 1946 (1)

"La Ruine de la Mère" (2)

Château Peut-Être d'Ecosse (3)

Castel en l'air des Sables d'Oran

Grande Cuvée Tamise Impériale (H_2O)

---

(1) Beer   (2) Gin   (3) Scotch Whisky?

Lord Mountbatten speaking at the Taj Palace dinner

1947

INDIAN INDEPENDENCE DINNER

SPICED CHICKEN CONSOMMÉ

·

HINDU DELICACIES

·

CHICKEN SOUFFLÉ

·

FRUIT AND MERINGUE

LONG FOUGHT FOR AND HARD won, India's independence from the UK officially commenced at the stroke of midnight on 15 August 1947. Hundreds of people gathered at the Gateway of India monument in Bombay, while at the city's Taj Palace Hotel, in honour of this event and the creation of Pakistan as an entirely separate nation, a dinner was hosted on the eve of emancipation. The three-course meal was both a reflection of the trends of the country's elite at the time, and a nod to patriotism – namely, haute-style French cuisine, punctuated with Indian spices. The dinner began with a spiced chicken consommé, 'Hindu delicacies', a chicken soufflé, and finally fruit and meringue. This was followed by speeches, various cabaret performances and, finally, a ballet. The dinner was attended by dignitaries and the aristocracy, including Lord Mountbatten, the last Viceroy of India. The following day, the city was alive with festivities, and public transport was made free for ease of people travelling around the city to celebrate.

LUNCHEON

CAVIAR FRAPPE

CONSOMME, JULIENNE

OMELET WITH WALNUT JELLY, STRIP OF BACON

SHRIMPS CREOLE, WITH FLUFFY STEAMED RICE

FRIED YOUNG CHICKEN, WHITE WINE-FLAVORED, AU SEC

BAKED SUGAR-CURED HAM, CHAMPAGNE SAUCE

GARDEN PEAS   CREAM-WHIPPED POTATOES

SOUTHERN PACIFIC SALAD BOWL

CORN BREAD   HOT ROLLS

ICE CREAM, SWEET WAFERS

HOT APPLE PIE WITH CHEESE

ASSORTED CHEESE, TOASTED WAFERS

CHILLED CRANSHAW MELON

COFFEE   TEA   MILK

The food offerings from the dining car

1959

KHRUSHCHEV'S CALIFORNIA RAILWAY DINNER

AS THE SUCCESSOR OF Joseph Stalin, and a declared devotee of his regime, Nikita Khrushchev's term as Soviet prime minister held both moments of coexistence and moments of crises in terms of the Soviet Union's relationship with the West. The latter is most commonly associated with the Cuban Missile Crisis in 1962, while the former is noted by his state visit to the US – the first by a leader of the Soviet Union.

On 15 September 1959, Khrushchev and his wife landed on American soil and were greeted by President Eisenhower. Supposedly a result of Vice President Nixon's gentle persuasion in regards to a US excursion when visiting the Soviet Union and Poland, the two-week visit was filled with intense talks and travel across the country, including California. This menu, offered to the Khrushchevs on their 13-hour train journey between Los Angeles and San Francisco, was written in both English and Russian. This is as far as compromise went, as the food on offer was decidedly American in style. Breakfast offerings included eggs and bacon and sliced fresh peaches, while lunch dishes included shrimps Creole, fried chicken, baked sugar-cured ham with Champagne sauce, southern Pacific salad bowl, and hot apple pie; vodka made an appearance in the form of a classic martini. On his visit to Hollywood, the leader met stars such as Marilyn Monroe, Frank Sinatra and Elizabeth Taylor – but a much-anticipated visit to Disneyland was cancelled as a result of security concerns.

Пожалуйста отмечайте, ✓ в указанном месте, каждое отдельное блюдо, которое вы хотите получить.

Please check ✓ in space provided the menu items you desire.

LUNCHEON   ЗАВТРАК

CAVIAR, FRAPPE
ИКРА FRAPPE

CONSOMME, JULIENNE
БУЛЬОН JULIENNE

☐ OMELET WITH WALNUT JELLY, STRIP OF BACON
ОМЛЕТ С ВАРЕЬЕМ, БЭКОН

☐ SHRIMPS CREOLE, WITH FLUFFY STEAMED RICE
КРЕВЕТКИ CREOLE С РИСОМ НА ПАРУ

☐ FRIED YOUNG CHICKEN,
WHITE WINE-FLAVORED, AU SEC
ЖАРЕНЫЕ ЦЫПЛЯТА В БЕЛОМ ВИНЕ, AU SEC

☐ BAKED SUGAR-CURED HAM, CHAMPAGNE SAUCE
ЗАПЕЧЕННАЯ ВЕТЧИНА, СОУС CHAMPAGNE

GARDEN PEAS   CREAM-WHIPPED POTATOES
ЗЕЛЕНЫЙ ГОРОШЕК
КАРТОФЕЛЬНОЕ ПЮРЕ

SOUTHERN PACIFIC SALAD BOWL
САЛАТ SOUTHERN PACIFIC

CORN BREAD   HOT ROLLS
КУКУРУЗНЫЙ ХЛЕБ, ГОРЯЧИЕ БУЛОЧКИ

☐ ICE CREAM, SWEET WAFERS
МОРОЖЕНОЕ, БИСКВИТЫ

☐ HOT APPLE PIE WITH CHEESE
ЯБЛОЧНЫЙ ПИРОГ С ЛОМТИКАМИ СЫРА

☐ ASSORTED CHEESE, TOASTED WAFERS
ОТБОРНЫЕ СЫРЫ, ВАФЛИ

☐ CHILLED CRANSHAW MELON
ДЫНЯ CRANSHAW СО ЛЬДА

☐ COFFEE   ☐ TEA   ☐ MILK
КОФЕ,   ЧАЙ,   МОЛОКО

Above: The order card presented with the menu

Opposite: The drinks menu presented to Khrushchev and his wife on their cross-country train

НАПИТКИ / BEVERAGES

ВИСКИ, ДЖИН, КОНЬЯК и др.: | **WHISKIES, GIN, BRANDIES, ETC.:**

ШОТДАНДСКАЯ заграничная	IMPORTED SCOTCH
КАНАДСКАЯ с бандеролью	CANADIAN, BONDED
BOURBON OR RYE, разлитая по бутылкам с бандеролью	BOURBON OR RYE, BOTTLED IN BOND
РОМ	RUM
ВОДКА	VODKA
ДЖИН домашнего производства	GIN, DOMESTIC
ВЫДЕРЖАННЫЙ КОНЬЯК лучшего качества	FINE OLD COGNAC BRANDY
КАЛИФОРНИЙСКИЙ КОНЬЯК	CALIFORNIA GRAPE BRANDY

КОКТЕЙЛИ: | **COCKTAILS:**

MANHATTAN	MANHATTAN
DRY MARTINI	DRY MARTINI
VODKA MARTINI	VODKA MARTINI
OLD FASHIONED	OLD FASHIONED

ЛИКЕРЫ: | **LIQUEURS:**

РАЗНЫЕ ЛИКЕРЫ	VARIETY OF LIQUEURS

ВИНА: | **WINES:**

ХЕРЕС ИЛИ ПОРТВЕЙН	SHERRY OR PORT

ПИВО и ALE | **BEER AND ALE**

МИНЕРАЛЬНЫЕ ВОДЫ и др.: | **MINERAL WATERS, ETC.:**

SHASTA WATER	SHASTA WATER
CANADA DRY WATER	CANADA DRY WATER
GINGER ALE	GINGER ALE
ROOT BEER	ROOT BEER
COCA-COLA	COCA-COLA
PEPSI-COLA	PEPSI-COLA
DR. PEPPER	DR. PEPPER
7-UP	7-UP
PLUTO WATER	PLUTO WATER
CALSO WATER	CALSO WATER
WHITE ROCK WATER	WHITE ROCK WATER
ВИНОГРАДНЫЙ СОК	GRAPE JUICE
ОРАНЖАТ	ORANGEADE
ЛИМОНАД	PLAIN LEMONADE
POLAND WATER «натуральная»	POLAND WATER (NATURAL)

INAUGURATION

LUNCHEON

JANUARY TWENTIETH

NINETEEN HUNDRED SIXTY-ONE

UNITED STATES SENATE RESTAURANT

UNITED STATES CAPITOL

1961

JFK'S INAUGURATION LUNCH

WHILE JFK'S PRE-INAUGURATION BALL – hosted by Frank Sinatra and attended by the elite of Hollywood, including Tony Curtis, Harry Belafonte, Mark Rothko, John Steinbeck, Ernest Hemingway and Ella Fitzgerald – was perhaps one of the glitziest parties the capital had ever seen, the lunch hosted at the White House after the event was a decidedly more homely affair. Political representatives from six states formed the hosting committee for the lunch, at which they were served American classics that reflected the comforts of country cooking with the odd touch of decadence: cream of tomato soup, New England lobster, Texas ribs of beef, string beans, and dinner rolls, with French-style pâtisserie to finish.

John F. Kennedy's presidency marked a time of both economic growth and global uncertainty with the continuation of the Cold War, and as a result, a swell of introspection. His inaugural statement – which includes 'My fellow Americans, ask not what your country can do for you, ask what you can do for your country. My fellow citizens of the world: ask not what America will do for you, but what together we can do for the freedom of man' – has become famous the world over. While his term lasted less than three years after his tragic assassination in 1964, his legacy as a statesman and an icon of American culture endures.

Opposite and overleaf: A menu from JFK's inauguration lunch, the cover featuring signatures of attendees, and the internal pages filled with the White House's offerings

In Honor of

The President of the United States

JOHN FITZGERALD KENNEDY

and

The Vice President of the United States

LYNDON BAINES JOHNSON

Supreme Court Chamber, Capitol Building

☆

Hosts

The Joint Congressional Inaugural Committee

JOHN SPARKMAN, of Alabama, *Chairman*

CARL HAYDEN, of Arizona

STYLES BRIDGES, of New Hampshire

SAM RAYBURN, of Texas

JOHN W. MCCORMACK, of Massachusetts

CHARLES A. HALLECK, of Indiana

INAUGURAL LUNCHEON 1961

Cream of Tomato Soup With Crushed Popcorn

Deviled Crabmeat Imperial

*New England Boiled Stuffed Lobster With
Drawn Butter*

Prime Texas Ribs of Beef au jus

String Beans Amandine   *Broiled Tomato*

*Grapefruit and Avocado Sections With
Poppyseed Dressing*

Hot Garlic Bread   *Butterflake Rolls*

Pattiserie Bâteau Blanche

Mints   *Coffee*

Barack Obama's place setting at his inaugural lunch

2009

BARACK OBAMA'S FIRST MEAL IN THE WHITE HOUSE

SEAFOOD STEW
·
BRACE OF AMERICAN BIRDS WITH VEGETABLE MEDLEY
·
CINNAMON APPLE SPONGE CAKE

AT BARACK OBAMA'S FIRST term inauguration lunch on 20 January 2009, the 230 guests at the White House were served a menu inspired by President Abraham Lincoln. It at once encapsulated the inherent optimism of this next chapter in American history, while also taking humble inspiration from the country's traditional home-style cooking.

The president's speech itself was among one of the most watched on record. Inspired by the phrase 'A New Birth of Freedom' from Lincoln's famous Gettysburg Address, the forty-fourth president spoke of hope and national unity before he and his guests sat down to a meal that celebrated American produce, where the names of dishes belied the visual elegance of the meal. Virginia-based catering company Design Cuisine, in an interview with *The Guardian* prior to the feast, stated that Obama had requested a meal that inspired '"comfort", not too elaborate, not too fancy.' The meal began with a favourite of Abraham Lincoln – seafood stew – made with Maine lobster, scallops, prawns and cod, topped with puff pastry. Next came came a fairly traditional -sounding offering of duck and pheasant with asparagus, carrots, Brussels sprouts and wax beans and pinot noir from California, followed by what can only be described as an all-American favourite – cinnamon and apple cake. The menu was sophisticated and crowd-pleasing in equal measure.

Air France Concorde advert

SOCIAL CHANGES THAT MADE MENUS

This section provides true food for thought; menus themselves can signify cultural shifts, politically divisive decisions and advancements in technology. These events, though extremely varied, all represent one thing – progression – and the food that defined them is no less important.

1918   American Red Cross Canteen Food

1933   Prohibition-Era Cocktails

1944   School Dinners

1948   The First NHS Hospital Food

1969   Eating in Space

1978   What Was Onboard Concorde?

Menu from a Red Cross canteen at the Front in France for a dinner on Lexington Day, given by staff of the French sector in honour of the American Red Cross Director

1918

AMERICAN RED CROSS CANTEEN FOOD

SANDWICHES

·

PIES

·

DONUTS

THE RED CROSS IN THE US initially functioned within the country, as a means of providing troops on the move between states with free meals and snacks, mainly existing at important travel junctions or railway stations. However, this enterprise soon spread to Europe once America joined the First World War in 1917. Beginning in Paris and serving American troops, the Red Cross quickly expanded to feed allied troops from Italy, France and the UK. According to the organisation, nearly 40 million troops from across the globe were served during the war by some 55,000 female volunteers. For these women, working for the Red Cross was seen as a calling; the 22 canteens that were positioned along the front lines were in highly dangerous locations, created in abandoned houses and sheds – essentially anything with a roof – with women making the food and men staffing the facilities.

The canteen service supplied sandwiches, cookies, cakes, biscuits, doughnuts and pies to hungry soldiers passing through, which boosted their rations – by then, fairly lean. In addition, bathroom facilities were provided, as well as seating areas for a moment's rest. The canteens were stationed on front lines, at aviation camps, in hospitals, and in cities where troops were continuously being transported in and out of Europe.

American Red Cross canteen worker serves coffee to US soldiers at Issoudun, 1918

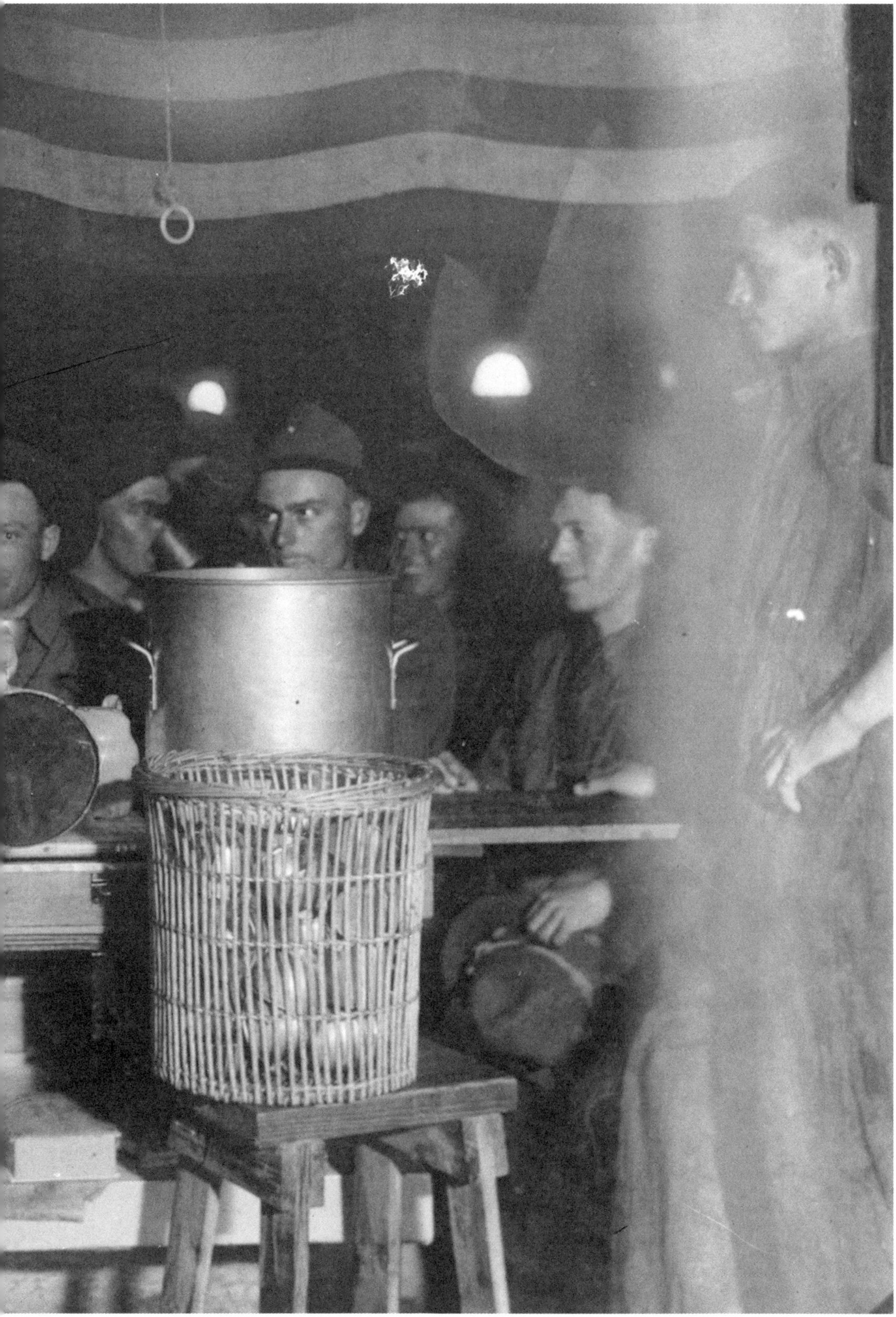

THE COMMODORE
NEW YORK

GRILL ROOM
Thursday, May 18, 1933
L U N C H E O N

Crab Flake Cocktail   Italian Antipasto

Potage Germiny   Chicken Algerienne

Celery

Omelette with Capon Livers
Baked Sea Trout with Salt Pork
Calf's Head, Vinaigrette, Russian Salad
Braised Second Joint of Turkey in Burgundy Wine
Chopped Sirloin Steak, Colbert
Fresh Vegetable Luncheon, Stuffed Green Pepper

New String Beans in Cream   Buttered Beets
Lyonnaise Potato   Mousseline Potato

Lettuce and Tomato Salad

Assorted Rolls   Melba Toast

Chocolate Soufflet Pudding, Cream Sauce
Apricot Pie   Banana Ice Cream   New England Apple

Tea   Coffee   Milk

12 to 2:30 P. M. $1.25

NO SUBSTITUTION OF DISHES

Lunch menu at the Grill Room of The Commodore, New York, 1933

1933

PROHIBITION-ERA COCKTAILS

WHILE AMERICA'S PROHIBITION ERA ironically heralded the invention of some of the most globally recognised cocktails – think mint julep, gin fizz, sidecar and whiskey sour – legend has it that it's also responsible for the creation of other types of cocktail: seafood, and fruit. Beginning in 1920 and lasting until 1933, the Eighteenth Amendment banned alcoholic drinks above 0.5% ABV. The rise of organised crime as a result of this legislation has been much documented and glamourised, but how did it affect the hotels, bars and restaurants that had built their enviable reputations through their drinks lists? Well, by encouraging them to find new ways of making money from their menus, now that alcohol mark-ups were off limits.

The seafood snack originated on the coast of California in the early twentieth century: shellfish such as prawns, lobster and crab, along with a spicy 'cocktail' sauce of ketchup, chilli and often horseradish, and a bit of lettuce was a way of creating a little flourish on a menu before a meal. It was also the perfect use for the elegant stemmed glassware that had now become redundant – as was a fruit cocktail. As a result, this alternative to aperitifs gained popularity. This menu from The Commodore Hotel (now named the Grand Hyatt) served a crab flake cocktail, while the Berkeley hotel in New York offered a fruit cocktail to kick off dinner proceedings.

A dinner lady serves lunch to schoolchildren, 29 October 1949

1944

SCHOOL DINNERS

SPAM FRITTERS

·

SHEPHERD'S PIE

·

JAM ROLY POLY

THE NATIONAL SCHOOL MEALS POLICY was introduced in 1944 through the Education Act, meaning that children in every school across the UK were offered free lunchtime meals and milk for the first time in history; the programme was fully rolled out by 1947. While food had been provided for poorer families since 1879, this was a positive step for society at a time of political reform under the shadow of the war. In an article in the *Dover Express*, the initiative was described as both 'popular and successful', with 'a different menu every day'. Indeed, it meant that 'the children have meals such as would be impossible on the home ration, liberal helpings of roast beef and Yorkshire pudding, or boiled mutton'.

In Dover, older children worked in rotation to help serve the meals, with food being cooked in the previous home economics centre. By the 1950s, school dinners had standardised somewhat, and so lunchtime staples became icons of British food culture over the decades: spam fritters, shepherd's pie, steamed sponges and custard, jam roly poly. While these meals might bring back feelings of horror for some, and have come under justifiable scrutiny in recent years, free food for all provided a much-needed step towards equality in education.

The National Health Service

HIS MAJESTY'S STATIONERY OFFICE   6d. NET

Front cover of an NHS booklet, 1947

1948

THE FIRST NHS HOSPITAL FOOD

MUTTON PIE

·

BOILED CABBAGE, SWEDE AND POTATOES

·

BAKED RICE WITH PEACH MELBA

THE NATIONAL HEALTH SERVICE, formed in 1948, was one of the most significant post-war social reforms to have been made in the UK's history. While today's hospital food is as diverse as the patients it's served to, meals back in the early days of the NHS were dictated by the recovering economy and food rationing – which was still in place until 1954, long after the war ended. Sugar, eggs, cheese, meat and tea were still rationed, while bread – never rationed during wartime – was actually introduced to the ration in 1946. Meals given to patients met the bare minimum of nutritional requirements by today's standards, and included dishes such as braised calves' head, kippers and vegetables grown in hospital gardens. As food was cooked on the premises in the 1940s, as opposed to being provided by a centralised supplier as it is today, meals were varied, but in general, reflected the home-cooked food of the era – protein and two veg, three if you were very lucky.

Despite trends changing over the last 70 or so years, one thing that has remained similar is breakfast – toast and porridge have never been off the menu, even if the days of sweetbreads and tinned fish are, thankfully, long gone.

Food kits used by NASA astronauts, including dehydrated fruit juices

1969

EATING IN SPACE

BACON SQUARES

·

SUGAR COOKIES

·

COFFEE

AMERICA'S MOON MISSION WAS perhaps one of the most historic events of the twentieth century; Neil Armstrong and Buzz Aldrin's journey in Apollo 11 resulted in the first manned landing, and, inevitably, the first meal eaten on the surface of the moon. But this wasn't the first dinner in space – that honour goes to astronaut John Glenn, who, in 1962, was unwittingly the guinea pig for the experiment of whether it was possible to eat at zero gravity. Luckily, it was, and so Glenn consumed a tube of apple sauce. Not perhaps the most appetising of meals, but a landmark nonetheless.

When it was the turn of Aldrin and Armstrong, it was a slightly more elaborate affair – dehydrated bacon squares, peaches, sugar cookies and a grapefruit-pineapple drink were on the menu, rounded off with a coffee. The meal took place at the Sea of Tranquility, and, after almost 22 hours on the surface of the moon, the astronauts jetted back to earth.

Although the technology behind space travel may have changed, the meals served have surprisingly not altered much – bacon is still on the menu, but now, astronauts pick from a menu of more than 100 items, sometimes months in advance.

Aperitifs and Cocktails

Sweet and Dry Vermouth
Campari Soda
Americano . Negroni
Medium Dry Sherry
Dry Martini . Gin . Vodka
Bloody Mary . Old Fashioned . Manhattan
Sours – *Whisky . Gin . Brandy*
Gin Fizz

Highballs – *Whisky . Brandy . Gin . Rum*

Champagne Cocktail

Spirits

Whisky – *Scotch . Bourbon . Rye*
Gin
Vodka

Beers

Ale . Lager

Selection of Soft Drinks

Wines

Champagne
Grand Siècle
or
Heidsieck Dry Monopole 1975

Bordeaux
Château la Dominique 1973
as available

White Burgundy
Chablis 1979

Liqueurs

Remy Martin Napoleon Brandy
Drambuie . Cointreau . Kahlua
Fonseca Bin 27 Port

Jamaica Macanudo cigars

Aperitifs — Champagne

Canapés
Caviar, goose liver pâté and shrimps

Lunch
Déjeuner

Saumon fumé et crabe
Thin slices of scotch smoked salmon garnished with crab legs presented with lemon and buttered brown bread

— * —

Tournedos grillé aux chanterelles
Prime fillet of beef seared on a hot griddle, served with sautéed cantharellus mushrooms

Pâté chaude de gibier
This English style game pie is prepared from marinated venison, pheasant, mushrooms and morels baked with a crust of flaky puff pastry

Truite Cléopâtre
A filleted trout, pan fried in butter, garnished with shrimps, capers and soft roes and finished with nut brown butter

Légumes
French beans, baby carrots and baked straw potatoes with artichokes

— * —

Salade
Wafers of avocado pear and apple, flavoured with lemon juice and fresh mayonnaise

— * —

Choix de fromage
A selection of French Camembert, English Stilton and Cheddar cheese

— * —

Fraises Romanoff
Ripe strawberries marinated in orange juice, flavoured with maraschino and kirsch, mixed with lightly whipped dairy cream

— * —

Café . Coffee
Served with chocolate mint crisps

Concorde menu from a London to New York flight, 1978

1978

WHAT WAS ONBOARD CONCORDE?

CAVIAR

·

BRITISH LAMB

·

STRAWBERRY VACHERIN

THROUGHOUT THE TWENTIETH CENTURY, travel, whether by air, sea or rail, inevitably gravitated towards touches of luxury as a result of preceding accessibility to innovation. Commercial flying remained somewhat elitist for many years after the first passenger trip in 1914, due in most part to prohibitive costs, but it was the advent of Concorde, and the onset of the 1980s economic boom, that took air travel to new levels of luxury.

Travelling at supersonic speed – twice the speed of sound, to be exact – Concorde, used by both British Airways and Air France, ferried more than 2.5 million passengers between 1976–2003, and cut the flying time between London and New York to just three and a half hours, compared to the standard eight hours.

Not only did Concorde have its own wine cellar, but passengers were given three-course meals that included lobster, foie gras and caviar, and were designed by chef greats such as Paul Bocuse, Michel Roux and Richard Corrigan. The lunch menu on the first flight between London Heathrow and John F. Kennedy International Airport in New York was, as expected, an extravagant affair: caviar, crab, British lamb and strawberry vacherin were offered with Champagne, followed by cigars and Cognac. But by the early 2000s, demand for flights, with tickets costing up to £8,000, had dwindled and so Concorde took its final flight in 2003.

Potato Pete, a popular figure in the UK's 'Dig for Victory' campaign during the Second World War

THE HISTORY OF COOKBOOKS

Despite their current cultural status — part memoir, part artistic expression, part coffee-table tome — cookbooks have historically had a much humbler place. These manuals reflected social change, from social mobility and colonial exploration to ethical diets and abstract art movements.

1845   Eliza Acton's Modern Cookery for Private Families

1854   Soyer's Cookery for the People

1861   Beeton's Book of Household Management

1864   Australia's First Cookery Book

1932   Futurist Cooking

1936   Good Housekeeping

1940   Wartime Menus

1960   Marguerite Patten's Cookery in Colour

1974   George Bernard Shaw's Vegetarian Cookbook

MODERN COOKERY,

FOR PRIVATE FAMILIES,

REDUCED TO A SYSTEM OF EASY PRACTICE,

IN A SERIES OF

CAREFULLY TESTED RECEIPTS,

IN WHICH THE PRINCIPLES OF

BARON LIEBIG AND OTHER EMINENT WRITERS

HAVE BEEN AS MUCH AS POSSIBLE APPLIED AND EXPLAINED.

BY ELIZA ACTON.

"It is the want of a scientific basis which has given rise to so many absurd and hurtful methods of preparing food."—Dr. Gregory.

NEWLY REVISED AND MUCH ENLARGED EDITION.
COPIOUSLY ILLUSTRATED.

LONDON:
LONGMANS, GREEN, READER, AND DYER.
1868.

The title page of the 1858 edition of Eliza Acton's now-famous work

1845

ELIZA ACTON'S MODERN COOKERY FOR PRIVATE FAMILIES

A BOILED LEG OF MUTTON WITH TONGUE AND TURNIPS

·

CHRISTMAS PUDDING

DESCRIBED BY DELIA SMITH as 'one of the best writers of recipes in the English language', Eliza Acton is largely undervalued, given the gravitas attached to her name in culinary circles past and present. Published in 1845, *Modern Cookery for Private Families* was one of the first thorough, comprehensive and adequately detailed cookbooks written in the UK. In its introduction, Acton boldly states what hundreds of food writers preceding her have turned into a mantra: 'good cookery is the truest economy'. In fact, Acton felt so strongly about the necessity of good food for the emerging middle class that she stated, 'it is from these classes that the men principally emanate to whose indefatigable industry, high intelligence and active genius, we are mainly indebted in our advancement in science, in art, in literature, and in general civilization'. Acton's tone throughout is one of borderline bombastic attention to detail, even including side notes for recipe titles. A boiled leg of mutton with tongue and turnips is suffixed with '(an excellent receipt [sic])', with a flourish of enthusiasm in the method: 'trim into handsome form a well kept but perfectly sweet leg of mutton'. The book is also the first reference to 'Christmas' pudding (as opposed to Dickens' 'plum' pudding) and a champion of British-style cooking, at a time when aspirational dining always had a French bent. But perhaps most importantly, Acton was one of the first to promote healthy, delicious and lovingly prepared food for everyone, no matter what their social status or budget.

Soyer's eyecatching cookbook cover

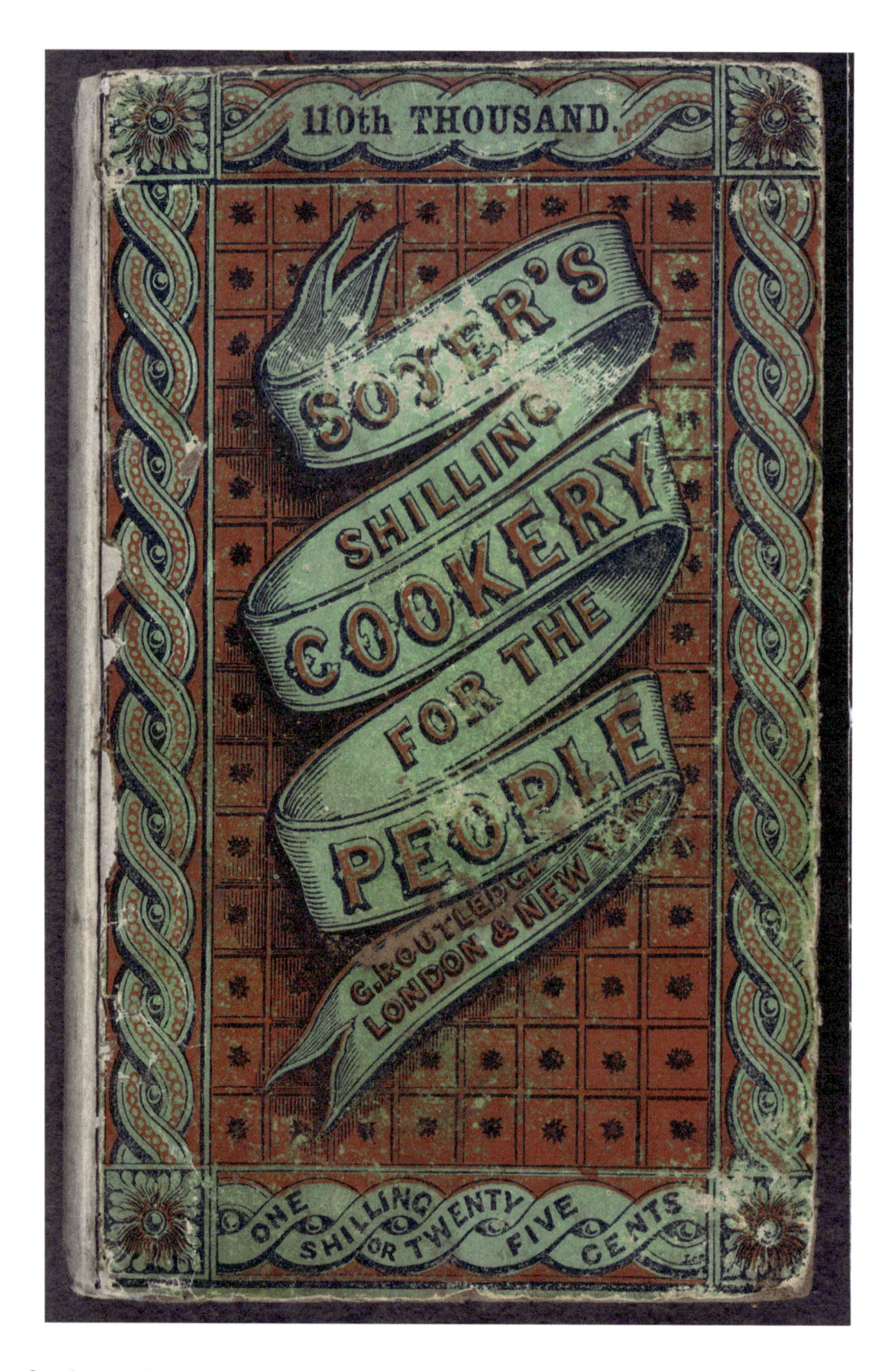

1854

SOYER'S COOKERY FOR THE PEOPLE

CHEAP PEA SOUP
·
SIMPLIFIED HODGE-PODGE
·
A PLUM PUDDING FOR THE MILLION

AT A TIME WHEN COOKERY writing focused heavily on the needs of the emerging middle classes – caught between the practical knowledge of their humbler roots and the now-expected airs and graces that came with wealth and social standing – Shilling Cookery for the People: An Entirely New System of Plain Cookery and Domestic Economy, written by Alexis Soyer in 1854, was a welcome tonic. Hailing from France, Soyer spent time in the kitchen of that country's dignitaries before cooking for royalty and nobility in England, garnering a reputation as an innovator. Soyer was renowned for his kitchen design, introducing cooking with gas, adjustable ovens and more efficient refrigeration systems to many households. However, he was also passionate about social justice, and in this sense, was a true progressive. It is said that he developed the concept of the 'soup kitchen', proposing to the British government that those affected by the famine in Ireland should be aided in this way – a project that was rolled out in Dublin in 1847. Having previously penned titles such as Soyer's Charitable Cookery and The Modern Housewife, Shilling Cookery was intended for those who were unable to afford kitchen equipment, or costlier ingredients. Heavily detailed, the book extols the virtues of oxtail for its nutritional content, fair price and ability to stretch to several meals, laments the inadequate use of herbs and salad leaves and subsequent food waste, and presents Soyer's recipe for a good-value plum pudding, 'adapted not for the millionaire, but for the million'. Recipes for Cheap Pea Soup and Simplified Hodge-Podge, a stew made with the offcuts of mutton, are deeply rooted in British tradition, but Soyer did add a French flourish, too – the book includes chapters on sauces and simple salads, and advocates the use of 'pints of butter'. Including illustrations of kitchen equipment, shortcut Christmas menus and even the recipes he developed for British Army camps in the Crimean War, what pervades in this vast swathe of recipes and writings is Soyer's passion for food, and for 'the people'; as he states, 'to eat without drinking, or to drink without eating, would soon send us to an early grave'.

3008.—WEDDING BREAKFAST FOR LARGE PARTY IN AUTUMN.

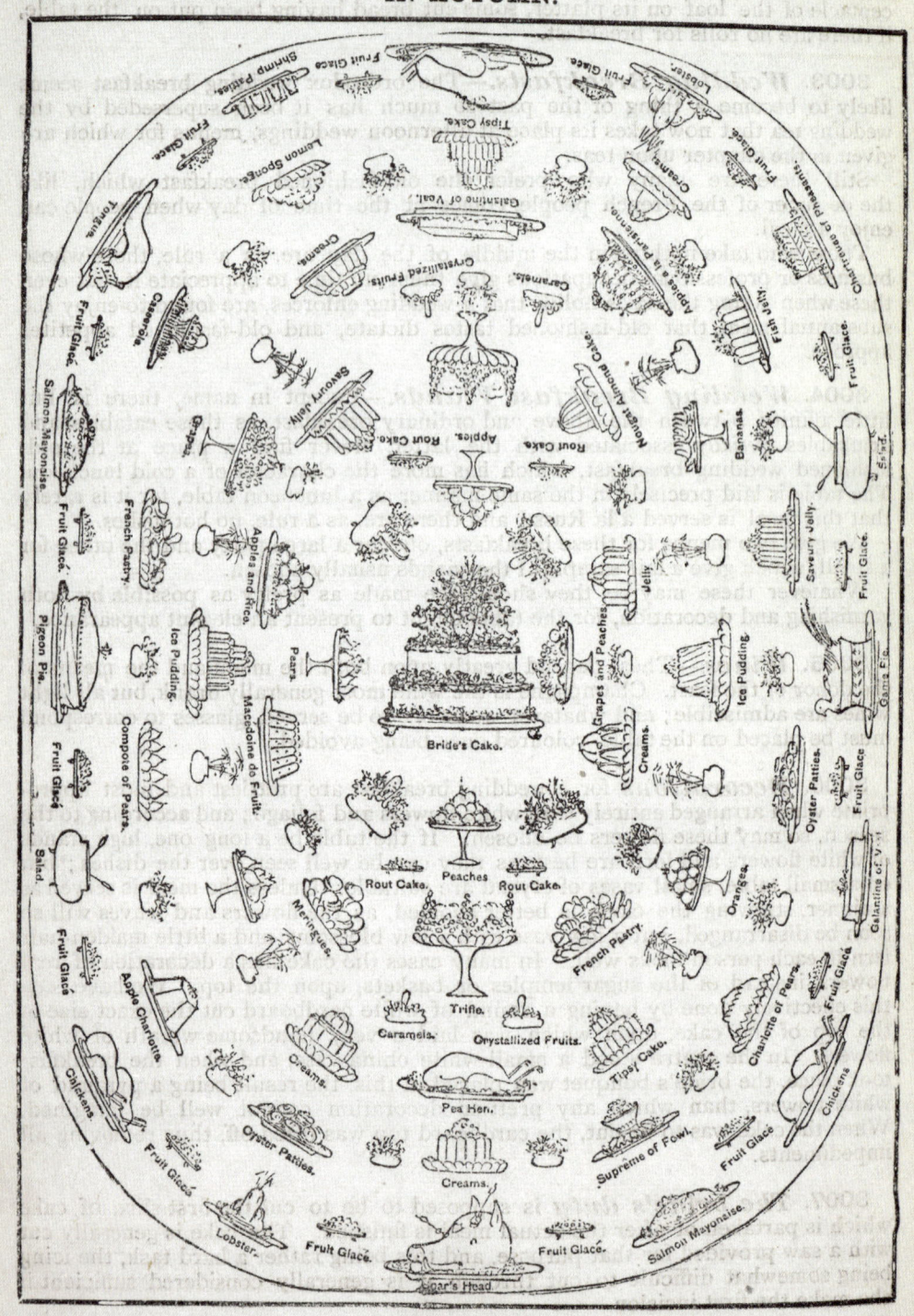

Note.—This breakfast is suitable for a very large party. The list of dishes, which can easily be reduced, will be found on page 1321.

Above: Illustration of a set table from *Beeton's Book of Household Management*
Overleaf: Dinner table set for 16

1861

BEETON'S BOOK OF HOUSEHOLD MANAGEMENT

LOBSTER SALAD
·
LITTLE PASTE CRUSTS WITH SWEETBREAD
·
ROAST BORDEAUX PIGEONS
·
SMALL HAM SOUFFLÉS
·
PUFFED POTATOES
·
GOOSEBERRY CREAM CHARLOTTE

BEETON'S BOOK OF HOUSEHOLD MANAGEMENT is arguably one of the most significant publications as a reflection of social history in the last 175 years. A tome now totalling more than 1,000 pages, it has sold over two million copies and is still in print today, despite the death of its author in 1865. The book was originally a 24-part magazine serial that Isabella Beeton began writing at just 21 years old, and which was published by her husband Samuel. Speaking about her motivation to create the work in the preface, she said, 'I have always thought that there is no more fruitful source of family discontent than a housewife's badly cooked dinners and untidy ways'. As a guide to everything from how to interview servants for household positions and whether to bring dogs on social outings to baking a perfect vanilla sponge and the most advisable cuts of meat for soup, it dictates the right way to go about any household task you could possibly think of. And menu planning is one of them. The menu suggestion above for a 'dainty luncheon' sounds anything but light by today's standards, including lamb offal, roasted game and the intriguing 'puffed potatoes'.

It was later discovered that Mrs Beeton lifted the majority of her recipes from other cookery books of time. Morally dubious, yes, but the result was a foolproof guide for the women of the emerging Victorian middle classes, who were navigating their way through previously inconceivable social mobility.

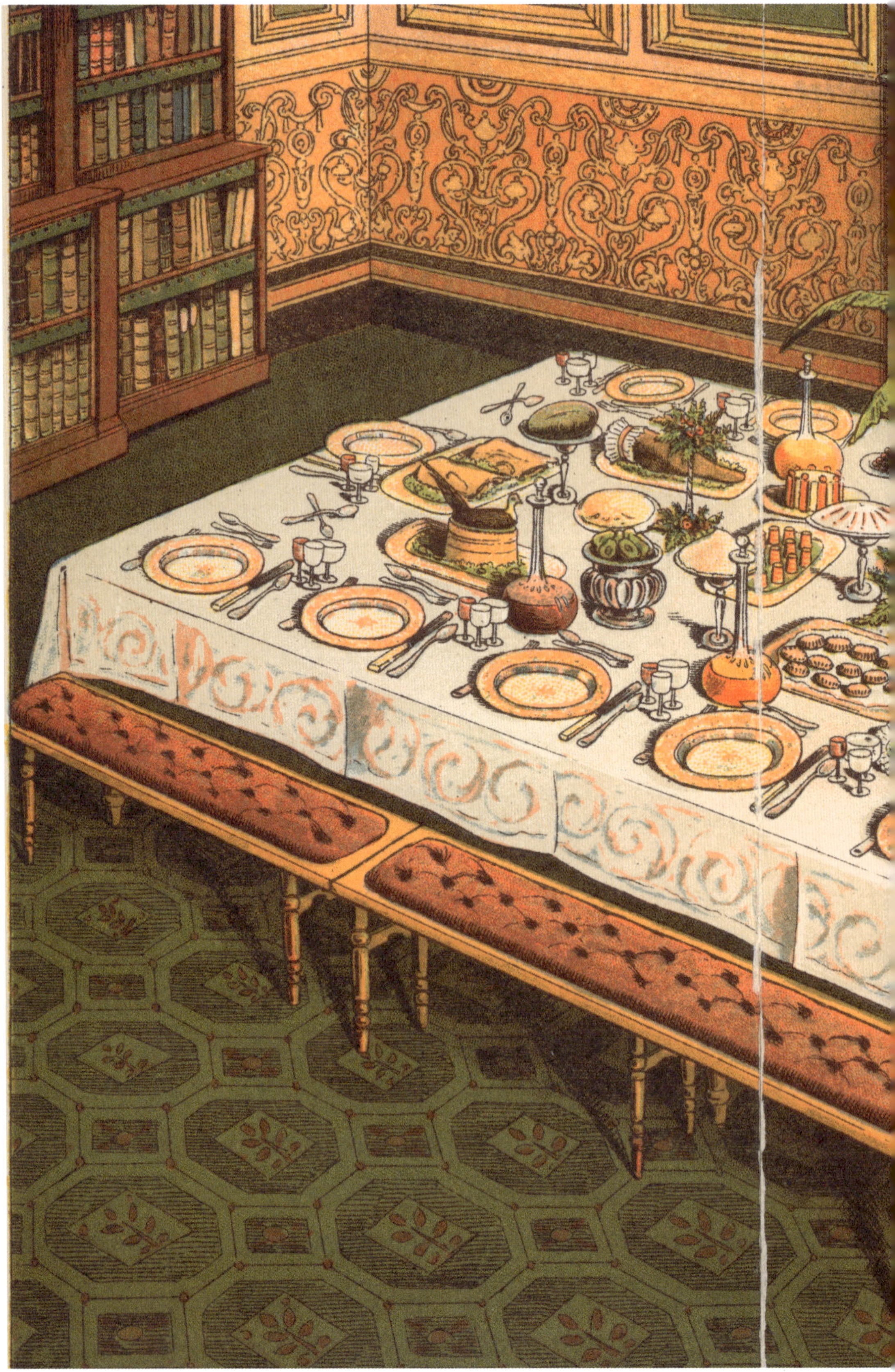

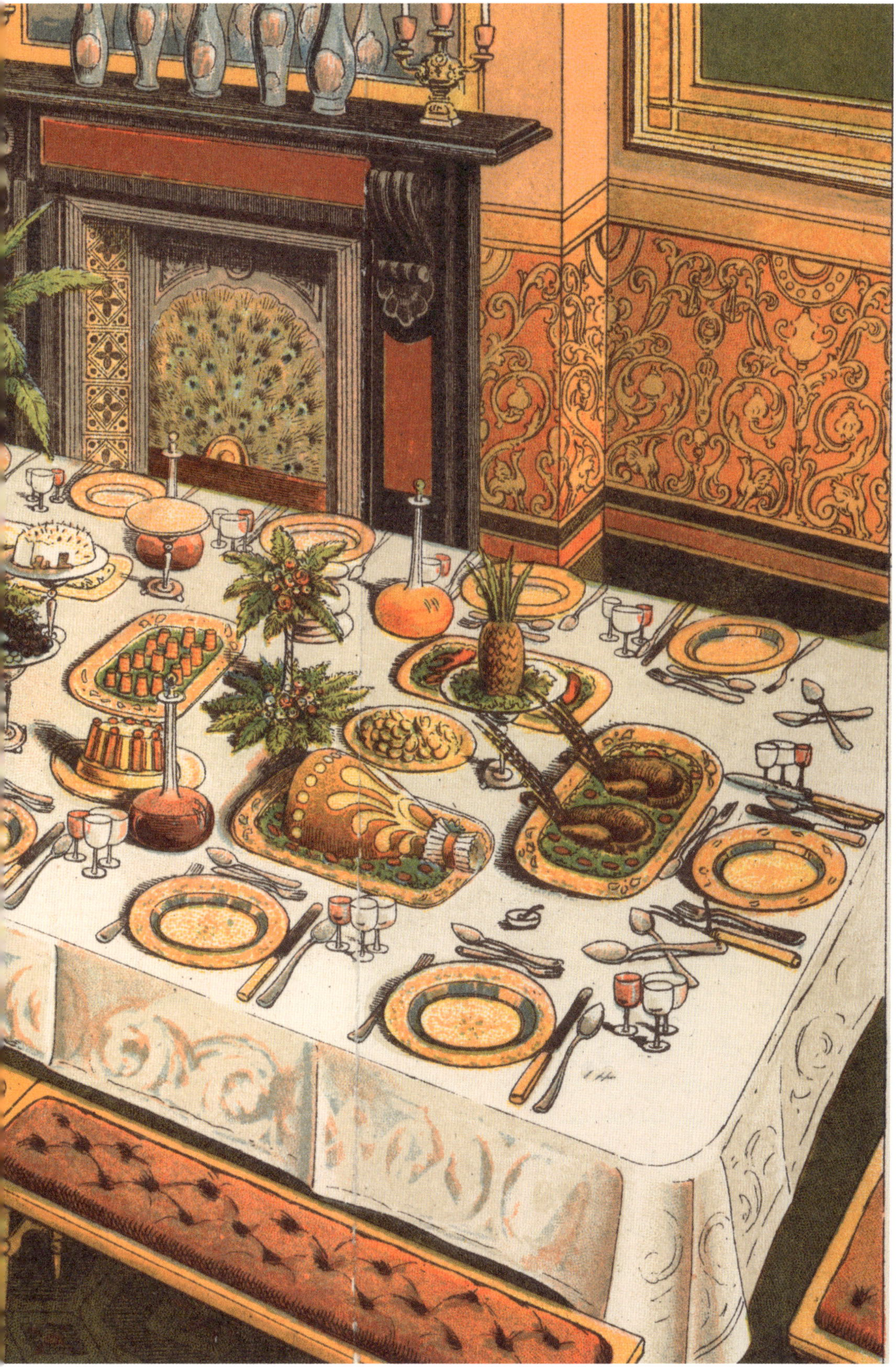

The title page of *The English and Australian Cookery Book*

1864

AUSTRALIA'S FIRST COOKERY BOOK

ROASTED WOMBAT

·

SHUV-IN-THE-MOUTH

·

SLIPPERY BOB

IN THE 1860S, AT THE SAME TIME as households in the UK were getting to grips with the rigorous instructions of *Beeton's Book of Household Management*, their Commonwealth cousins in Australia were about to be introduced to their own national culinary tome – the catchily titled *The English and Australian Cookery Book: Cookery for the Many, as Well as the Upper Ten Thousand*, written by Tasmanian farmer Edward Abbott. In what could arguably be the earliest example of the fusion food with which the Antipodean nation has now become synonymous, Abbott's recipes took the principles of European cooking, preserving and distilling and applied them to native animals and ingredients. The results? Roasted wombat, lard preserved with molasses, and 'shuv-in-the-mouth', a concoction of brandy, water and sugar, among 1,000 other recipes.

Abbott, born in Sydney, was passionate in his mission to provide inspiration for even the least fortunate, and hoped to document his local ingredients in their best light, even including a chapter on scraps to reduce food waste, and preparations for every part of the kangaroo – including the tail. The book, initially printed by a London-based publisher, was reprinted in 2014 to coincide with its 150th anniversary; unsurprisingly, the recipes garnered a lot of attention, specifically one for 'slippery bob' – kangaroo brains cooked in emu fat.

Cover of *The Futurist Cook Book*, 1932

1932

FUTURIST COOKING

CUBIST VEGETABLE PATCH
·
IMMORTAL TROUT
·
DATES IN MOONLIGHT

A CONTROVERSIAL MOVEMENT SPEARHEADED by artist Filippo Tommaso Marinetti in the early twentieth century, Futurism was a rejection of history and tradition in favour of the future – an exploration of the unknown, and fast-developing technologies. But how did this relate to food?

In 1930, Marinetti, along with Futurist painter Fillìa, developed the *Manifesto of Futurist Cooking*, which was followed in 1932 by *The Futurist Cookbook*. In effect, the latter was a rule book that championed the rejection of tried and tested combinations of food in favour of dishes that would both challenge and excite the imagination, from ingredients to presentation. There were 11 key requirements needed to meet the Futurist brief, which included: accompanying meals with perfume and music, to be changed with every course; the forgoing of knives and forks; the use of technology to ease preparation of dishes; and finally, the most widely contested suggestion, the abolition of pasta from the diet. Marinetti also recommended banning chat about politics at the dinner table – perhaps one of the book's wiser suggestions. Menus included a Cubist representation of an allotment, where vegetables were finely diced to no more than one cubic centimetre; fish dishes, such as 'Immortal Trout' – consisting of a fish stuffed with nuts, wrapped in calves' liver and then fried, to challenge the palate; and finally, desserts like 'Dates in Moonlight', consisting of ricotta laced with date purée, chilled until ready to serve, sound positively appetising.

Photograph of the first Futurist meal

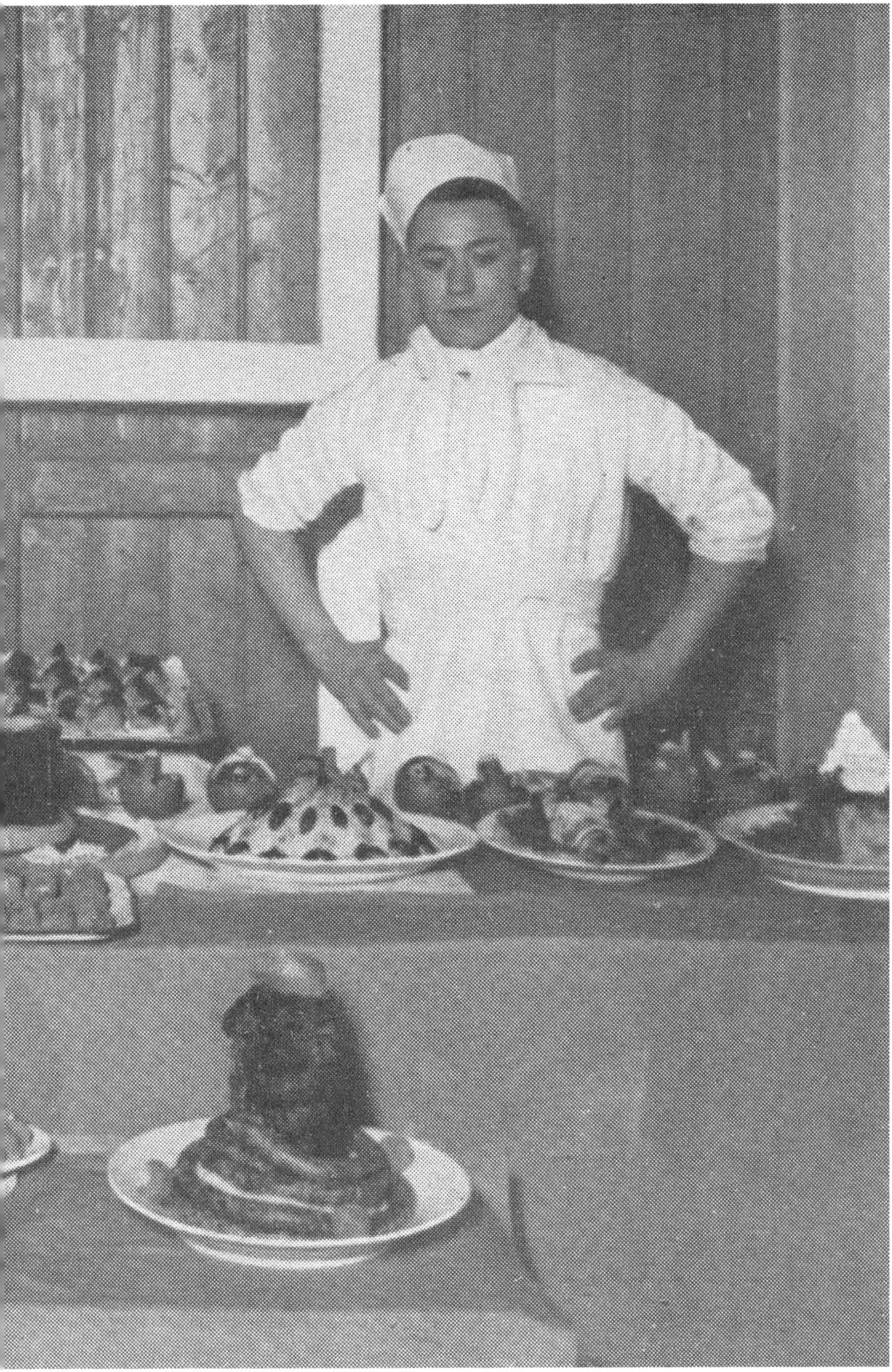

Autumn food from the *Good Housekeeping Book of Menus*, 1954

1936

GOOD HOUSEKEEPING

SALMON, SPAGHETTI AND TOMATO CASSEROLE

·

BUTTERED CORN

·

HEATED ROLLS

·

PINEAPPLE AND RED APPLE SALAD

·

ASSORTED CHEESES & CRACKERS

·

TEA

FROM ITS HUMBLE ROOTS as a fortnightly magazine produced in the US state of Massachusetts, *Good Housekeeping* has become something of a global institution over the last 134 years. Intended as a guide for women to navigate domestic matters – cooking, trends, products, and of course, housekeeping – the magazine boasted in excess of 300,000 readers in just a few short years.

In the early 1900s, the advent of electricity meant that households were transformed, with new electrical products on hand to make life easier and tasks quicker. As a reaction to this, *Good Housekeeping* set up what is now known as the GHI, or Good Housekeeping Institute, a lab where appliances are tested and rated for readers.

The magazine's content was always an indicator for social change, from the dangers of quick-fix diets in 1914, to campaigning for more federal funding for maternity care. Indeed, food editor Dorothy Marsh's article 'Dinners without Delay for Busy and Business Housekeepers' was a reaction to the increasing number of women going out to work. Both economical and practical, Marsh's menus heralded a social change that was to preclude the likes of fast food, drive-ins and TV dinners that are now synonymous with 1950s America. In her 1936 article, her top tips included mixing ready-to-serve items with cooked-from-scratch foods; organising menus at the beginning of the week; cooking extra potatoes and vegetables, to be used over two meals; and putting food straight onto plates, to avoid additional washing up from serveware – all sound advice.

PARTY MENUS

DINNER PARTY 1
Consommé Julienne
Roast Pheasant
Bread Sauce   Fried Crumbs
Game Chips
Green Salad with Tangerines
Peach Liqueur Flan

DINNER PARTY 2
Oxtail Soup
Fried Scallops
Grilled Beefsteak
Hot Potato Salad
Sauté of Peas
Strawberry Mousse
Sponge Fingers
Cheese Meringues

DINNER PARTY 3
Glazed Paupiettes of Sole
Roast Duck
Green Peas   Roast Potatoes
Apple Sauce   Orange Salad
Chocolate Refrigerator Cake
Angels on Horseback

CHRISTMAS DINNER 1
Artichoke Soup
Roast Turkey
Sausages   Bread Sauce
Brussels Sprouts
Christmas Pudding
Brandy Butter
Mince Pies

CHRISTMAS DINNER 2
Cream of Chestnut Soup
Turkey Soufflé Pie
Mushroom Fritters
Potato Croquettes
Flaming Peaches
Lemon Meringue Pie

NEW YEAR BUFFET
Ragoût of Goose with Chestnuts
Prawn Patties
Chicken and Tongue in Aspic
Asparagus Rolls
Nut and Cherry Trifle
Fruit Salad and Peach Ice Cream
Pineapple Sponge
Individual Trifles
Apricots in Liqueur
Petits Fours

DINNER PARTY 4
Marrow Cream Soup
Chicken and Ham Vol-au-Vent
Asparagus à la Crème
Lyonnaise Potatoes
Orange Soufflé
Bananas au Rhum
Sardine Strips

DINNER PARTY 5
French Tomato Soup
Salmon Trout Mayonnaise
Roast Parsley Potatoes
Summer Salad   Beetroot Salad
Cherry Flan   Baked Alaska

Dinner Party menus and images from the *Good Housekeeping Book of Menus*, 1954

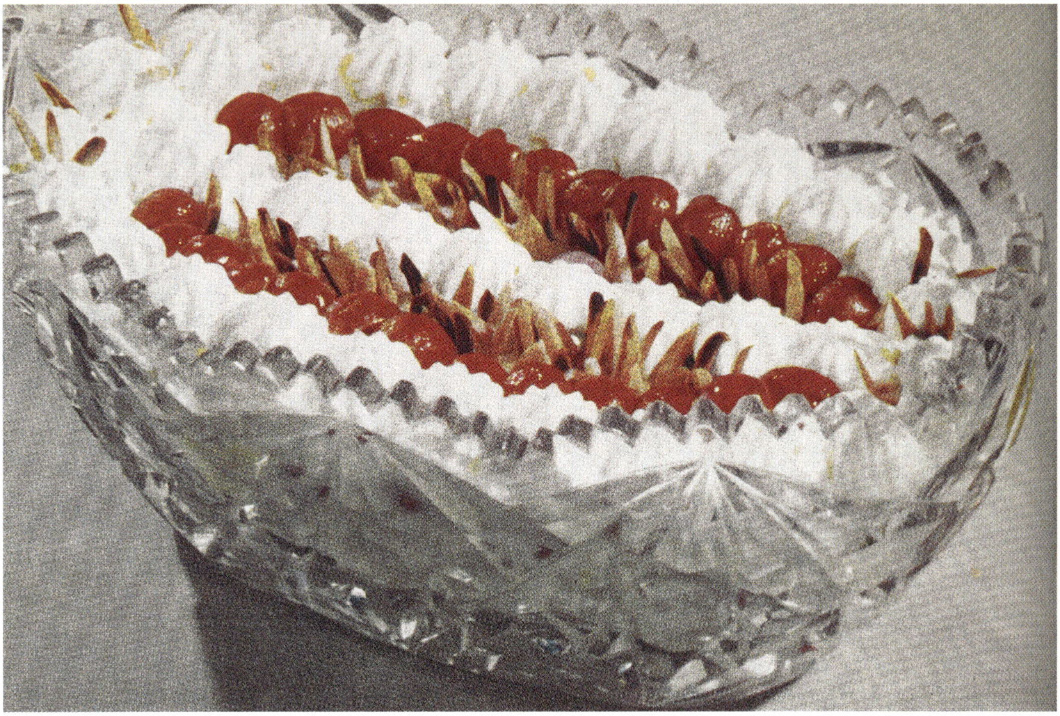
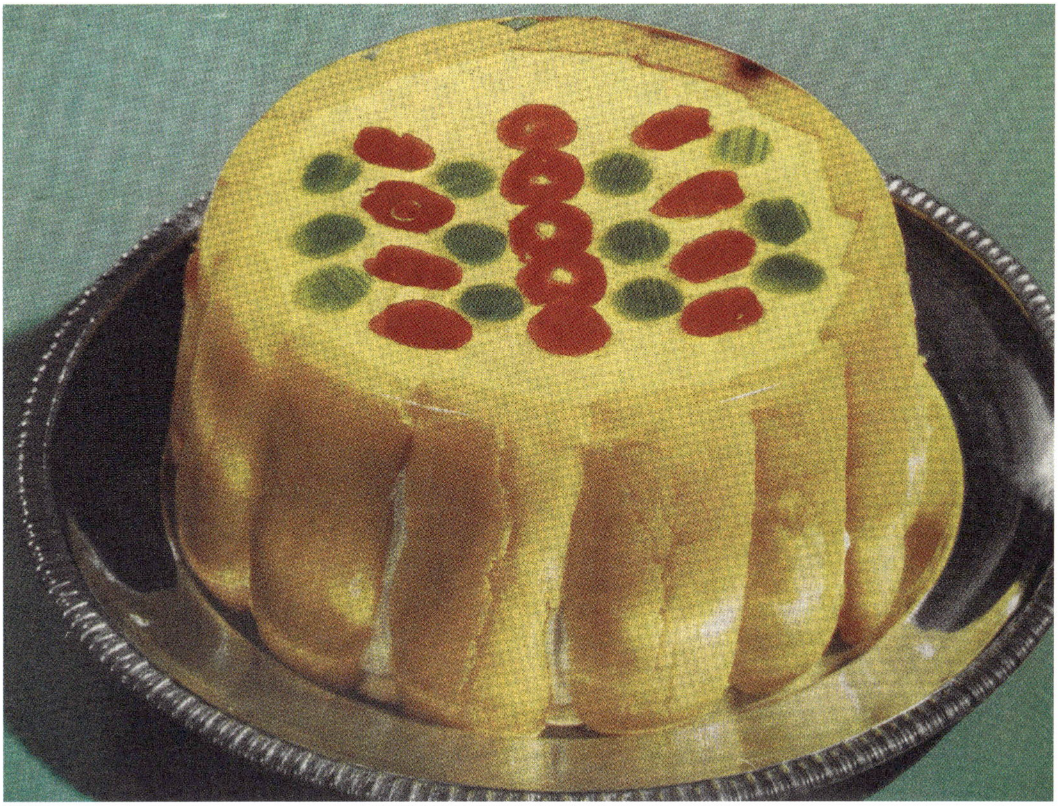

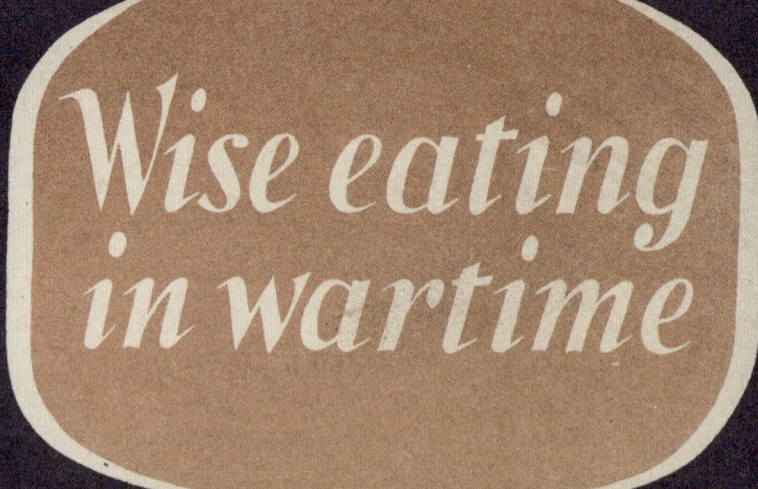

An advert for 'Wise Eating in Wartime', the Ministry of Food

1940

WARTIME MENUS

BACON HOT POT

·

SHREDDED CABBAGE

·

DUMPLINGS WITH SYRUP

AS A RESULT OF GERMANY'S strategy in the Battle of the Atlantic – attacking ships carrying imported goods bound for Britain – the Ministry of Food implemented a system of rationing certain foods across the UK in 1939, which remained in place for some ingredients for 15 years. Homegrown vegetables and bread were unlimited, but meat and dairy products such as bacon, other red meats and butter were heavily restricted, as was sugar. Eventually, cheese, eggs, tea, coffee, biscuits and canned fruit followed suit by 1942. As a result, the government published a series of leaflets to assist people in being creative with their limited supplies: filling out dishes with potatoes and vegetables, using stale bread in desserts and savoury dishes to ensure nothing went to waste, and using jam and golden syrup as a sweetener instead of sugar. The way meals were composed changed quite radically, and has had a lasting impact through to today; dumplings made with scant fat and golden syrup for sweetness found themselves on school dinner menus for decades to come. The recipes written by the Ministry provided content for hundreds of leaflets, and have had a lasting effect on British cooking to this day.

The menu overleaf from Maison Prunier, a French-style bistro in central London, clearly flags which foods on their menu are rationed (so only one per person can be ordered) and those that are not rationed and can therefore be enjoyed freely. They also offer an 'Air Raid Lunch' and a 'black-out taxi service' to get patrons home safe through Blitz-era London's darkened streets.

MENU

NO COVER CHARGED
(AUCUN PLAT N'EST SERVI POUR DEUX)

HORS d'OEUVRE

A LONDRES
MAISON PRUNIER
St. James's Restaurant Ltd
72 St. James's Street
Telephone Regent 1373-1374

TASTE OUR WINES
by glass
Anjou, Graves, Maconnais 1/9
Bordeaux Rouge 1/9
Champagne St. James 3/-

COQUILLAGES ET HUITRES

NOS SPECIALITES
Huitres Frites........ les 3 2/9
„ au Gratin..... „ 2/9
„ sur croûton.... „ 2/9
„ à l'Américaine „ 2/9
„ en Brochette.. „ 2/9
Potage aux Huitres...... 6/-
Variété Prunier (6 oysters) 5/6
Potage de Fruits de Mer 4/6

Bigorneaux............la portion 1/-
Moules Parquées.......la douz. 1/6
Portugaises ....la douz. 5/6
L'Assiette Saintongeaise 3/6
L'Assiette Blackout or Air Raid 3/6

Brittany petites.........la douz. 7/-
Brittany supérieures.... „ 9/6
Natives petites......... „ 8/-
Natives supérieures..... „ 10/-
Natives extra........... „ 12/-
(See full explanations on other page.)

PRUNIER SPECIAL GREEN OYSTERS
Petites 8/-
Supérieures 10/-
Extra 11/6

FUMAISONS, COCKTAILS
Saumon fumé.................3/-
Crevette Cocktail............3/-
Crabe Cocktail................3/-
Oyster Cocktail...............3/6

LE PLATEAU PRUNIER
Petit Sandwich Beurre d'Anchois
Petite Coquille salade de Crabe
Petite Coquille Crevettes Paprika
Petite coquille, sauce verte...
Fine Bouche de Saumon Fumé

CAVIAR
Caviar de Saumon... la cuiller... 3/6
Caviar Pressé......................... 4/6
Caviar Frais Russe Sevruga..... 7/-
Caviar Frais Russe Oscietre..... 9/-
Sandwich de Caviar Frais....... 1/3

DIVERS
Terrine de Lièvre...............3/6

Foie Gras à la Gelée de Porto 5/-

COQUILLAGES AND CRUSTACES
FROIDS
Potted Shrimps.......la portion 2/6
Bouquet................ „ 3/-

CHAUDS
St. Jaques Prunier...............3/6
St. Jaques Marinière.............4/-
St. Jaques Rochelaise............4/-

Crabe Mexicaine.................3/-
Crabe Dressé Mayonnaise.....4/-
MOULES MARINIÈRE.........3/-
Pilaff de Moules au Curry....3/6
Pilaff de Crabe Américaine...4/6
Pilaff de Crevettes Valencienne 4/6

Petit Homard Rémoulade........ 4/6
½ Langouste Mayonnaise......... 5/6
Homard Thermidor.....(1 per.) 5/-
Homard Grillé........................ 5/6
Homard Américaine................ 5/6
Homard Newburg................... 6/-

OEUFS
Œuf en Gelée..................1/9

Omelette au Caviar.......... 3/9

POTAGES
Consommé Celestine.........1/9

Bisque de Homard..............2/6
Soupe aux Moules..............2/6

Potage Parisienne.............. 2/6

Not Rationed

Only one dish can be selected from these items.

BY AGREEMENT WITH THE MINISTRY OF FOOD, ONLY ONE DISH OF MEAT OR POULTRY, OR GAME OR FISH MAY BE SERVED AT A MEAL (MEAT INCLUDING OFFALS) AND BE SELECTED FROM THE FOLLOWING ITEMS:

POISSON
Le Poisson du Chef ......See "TODAY"
STEAK DE TURBOT PARISIENNE 4/-

Hareng Grillé Sce. Moutarde ...2/6
Whitebaits Diables 3/-
Merlan Crawford 3/-

Grillade au Fenouil 4/-
BOUILLABAISSE..................4/6
Raie au Beurre Noir............3/6
Truite Meunière..................4/-

Barbue au Four 4/-

Sole Grillée 5/9
Filets de Sole Prunier 5/9

ENTREES, GRILLADE ET ROTS
Le Plat du Gourmet..........."See TODAY"

2 Côtes d'Agneau 3/6
Côte de Mouton ou Veau..... 4/-
Rognons Grillés Vert-Pré..... 3/6

Pilaff de Volaille au Curry.... 3/6
½ Poularde au Riz Suprême (2 pers) 12/-

Entrecôte Minute 4/-
Tournedos Beurre d'Anchois .. 4/6
Filet Boston (6 Huitres)....... 7/-

(Toutes les Grillades sont garnies Pommes Bataille)

GIBIER
Perdreau Rôti 10/6
Bécasse Flambée 12/6
Faisan Rôti 15/-

½ Perdreau aux Choux......... 5/6
Canard Sauvage au Porto.... 12/-
„ „ à la Presse... 15/-

Civet de Lièvre................... 4/6
Rable de Lièvre Sce. Poivrade 10/-

FROIDS
Langue 2/6
Jambon Froid 2/6

Mayonnaise de Volaille St. James 3/6

Poulet, la cuisse................. 5/6
Poulet, l'Aile...................... 6/6

LEGUMES
Haricots Verts au Beurre 2/-
Purée d'Epinards 2/-

Choux Fleurs Sautés 2/-

Petits Pois Etouffés Française 2/-
Champignons Grillés Sur Toast 2/6

Salade de Saison:............... 1/3

Salade Panachée, Salade M-C-B 1/6

Salade de Légumes............. 2/-

FROMAGES
Cheddar, — Cheshire 1/3 — Stilton 1/6 — A SPECIALITY; Cœur Mousseline 1/6

Not Rationed

ENTREMETS ET DESSERTS
Pôt de Crème; Chocolat, Vanille 1/6
Fruits Rafraîchis au Marasquin 2/6
Tarte aux Fruits.................. 2/6

Glace Vanille ou Fraise 2/-
Mousse Glacée Chocolat..... 2/3
Mousse Glacée au Rhum..... 2/6

Coupe Jack 2/6
Crêpes à l'Orange 3/6
Poire Nelusko 3/6

FRUITS DE SAISON
GRAPE FRUIT 1/6   POIRE 2/-

CAFE FILTRE 1/-   CAFE DECAFEINE 1/3

Open the Whole Year round — on Sundays for Lunch a 12-30, Dinner at 7
"TOUT CE QUI VIENT DE LA MER — EVERYTHING COMING FROM THE SEA"

Wartime menu from Maison Prunier

A few explanations about some French names on the Menu

OYSTERS
Brittany Petites and Supérieures: French Oysters re-laid in English Waters **Natives:** English bred Oysters
Prunier Green Special: Oysters bred in England but very similar to French Green Marennes
Assiette Saintongeaise: 6 small Brittany served with a hot sausage. **Portugaises:** Portuguese oysters re-laid in England
Assiette Black-out or Air Raid: 3 Portuguese – 3 small Brittany

COCKTAILS
Crevettes Cocktail: Shrimp Cocktail   **SHELLFISH**   **SMOKED FISH**
Crabe Cocktail: Crab Cocktail   **Bigorneaux:** Winkles   **Saumon Fumé:** Smoked Salmon
Moules Parquées: Raw Mussels

CAVIAR
Caviar de Saumon: Made with Salmon Roes   **Caviar Russe Sevruga:** Fresh Caviar but with smaller eggs than Oscietre
Caviar Pressé: Pressed Caviar   **Caviar Russe Oscietre:** Bigger egg caviar

DIVERS
Terrine de Lièvre: Hare Pâte
Foie Gras à la Gelée de Porto: Goose Liver served with jelly made with Port and Truffles

Not Rationed {

CRUSTACES
Crabe Mexicaine: Crab meat, lettuce served in crab shell
Crabe Dressé Mayonnaise: Dressed Crab   **Langouste:** Crawfish   **Bouquet:** Prawns
Pilaff: Rice cake stuffed with Crab, or Shrimps or Mussels and served with American, Newburg, Valencienne or Curry Sauce.
Homard Thermidor: Lobster Meat, Truffles, Mushroom Sauce on half Lobster shell.
Homard Newburg: Lobster with Cream Sauce Sherry, Truffles   **Homard grillé:** Broiled Lobster.
St. Jacques Prunier: Scollops served in a shell with cream sauce   **Marinière:** Scollops with white wine sauce, Shallot and Parsley
Rochelaise: Served in a shell with the same butter as for Snail
Moules Marinière: Mussels cooked with white wine, chopped onions and Parsley

EGGS
Oeuf en gelée: Egg enrobed in Jelly.
Omelette Caviar: Omelette with caviar.

SOUPS
Consommé Celestine: Consommé relieved with chopped pancakes   **Bisque de Homard:** Lobster Soup hot or cold
Soup aux Moules: Mussel soup   **Potage de Fruits de Mer:** Cream soup with cooked Oysters, Mussels
Potage Parisienne: Leaks and Potatoe Soup

FISH Cold Dishes
Steak de Turbot Parisienne: Cold Turbot in Jelly served with Tomatoes, Vegetable Salad

FISH Hot Dishes
Hareng Grillé Sauce Moutarde: Grilled Herring served with Hollandaise sauce, with slight a mixture of mustard
Grillade au Fenouil: Common fish grilled with fennel in front of client, as prepared in the South of France.
Raie au Beurre Noir: Skate cooked in burnt butter
Bouillabaisse: A variety of Fish with Tomatoes and Saffron Sauce.
Barbue au Four: Brill with White Wine and Cream Sauce
Sole Grillée: Grilled Sole served with melted butter
Filets de Sole Prunier: Sole, Poached Oysters, Truffles, Sauce with White Wine and Cream
Varieté Prunier: A selection of Oysters cooked in 6 different ways served in shells

Rationed {

MEAT AND POULTRY
Poularde au Riz Suprême: Boiled Chicken, its stock thickened with Cream, served with rice.
Tournedos au Beurre d'Anchois: Tournedos served with butter mixed with Anchovy Sauce.
Filet Boston: Tournedos with Oysters and Hollandaise Sauce   **Pilaff de Volaille au Curry:** Rice Cake stuffed with Chicken Curry Sauce
Mayonnaise de Volaille St. James's: Sliced Chicken with Mayonnaise, Lettuce Salad, Tomatoes, Eggs and Olives

GAME
Perdreau Rôti: Roast Partridge
Demi Perdreau aux Choux: ½ Partridge served with cabbage, sausage and bacon
Civet de Lièvre: Jugged Hare   **Râble de Lièvre:** Roast Saddle of Hare served with mashed chestnuts and Marinade Sauce
Canard Sauvage au Porto: Wild duck served with a port sauce
    " à la Presse: to replace the French Rouennais à la Presse served with cooked apples and chipped potatoes
Bécasse Woodcock singed with Brandy

VEGETABLES
Purée d'Epinards: Mashed Spinach   **Choux Fleurs:** Cauliflowers
Not Rat- **Haricots Verts:** French Beans.   **Laitue:** Lettuce   **Petits Pois:** Peas
Salade Panachée: a variety of salad or Lettuce with Eggs and Tomatoes   **Champignons:** Mushrooms
ioned **Salade M-C-B:** Mixture of corn salad, beetroot and Celery

SWEETS
Crêpes a l'Orange: Pancakes similar to Crêpe Suzette cooked with butter and orange, a drop of Triple Sec Liqueur.
Poire Nelusko: A pear served on a lid of vanilla ice dressed with hot chocolat sauce

When at Prunier ask for particulars of:–

Treasure Trove in Tins – Prunier's Specialities in tins for Home and Abroad – see leaflet

On Prendra ("One Will Take") Service see tariff – REGent 2615.

Air Raid Lunch 8/6   -   -   { 4 COURSES INCLUDING
Black - Out Dinner (from 6 p.m.) 10/6 { Oysters

BLACK-OUT TAXI SERVICE AVAIVABLE TO AND FROM PRUNIER'S

Open on Sundays for Lunch at 12-30 and Dinner – 7 p.m.

Cover of Patten's *Cookery in Colour*, 1960

1960

MARGUERITE PATTEN'S COOKERY IN COLOUR

DEVILS ON HORSEBACK
·
ANGELS ON HORSEBACK
·
CHEDDAR FINGERS
·
HAT PINS

TODAY, IT'S A GIVEN THAT cookbooks are filled with beautifully presented, vibrant photographs of the recipes inside – a guideline that verges on unattainable aspiration for the home cook. But before British food writer Marguerite Patten's seminal book, *Cookery in Colour*, was published in 1960, these books were predominantly text pages, with the odd illustration in black and white. In that sense, it was a book that changed everything – by 1969, it had sold more than one million copies. This was not, however, Patten's first foray into writing recipes that made a mark. During the Second World War, she developed recipes for the Ministry of Food, advising the country on how to make the most of meagre rations, including scrambled eggs with vegetables, corned-beef fritters and mock duck. Published by Hamlyn, *Cookery in Colour* was a tome of 1,000 recipes and techniques, a self-declared 'encyclopedia for every occasion'. As Patten deftly noted in the introduction 'the success of a meal lies in its appeal to the eye. Food should both taste and look good.' In the chapter on entertaining, a menu of cheddar fingers, sausage rolls and the curiously named 'hat pins' highlights just that.

PARTY FARE WITHOUT COOKING

1054 SANDWICHES WITH A DIFFERENCE

Never say sandwiches are dull. This picture shows a variety of sandwiches which are suitable even for the most special occasion.

Try: *Sandwich cones* Fresh bread moulded round cream horn cases. Fill with soft cheese, decorated with nuts and sliced olives, and garnish with salami slices

Card Sandwiches Bread cut into fancy shapes with a pastry cutter

Make sure your bread is fresh, and the filling moist. Press top and bottom layer of bread firmly together so that the sandwich does not come apart.

By itself, a plate of sandwiches does not look very exciting. But garnishes can make all the difference. Instead of the conventional parsley try halved tomatoes, mandarin oranges, watercress, prawns, cocktail onions, radish flowers — with suitable sandwiches all these garnishes look attractive and can be eaten too.

Serve a light white wine or fruit cup with a sandwich

Party menus from *Cookery in Colour*

1055 HAT PINS

8 oz. sausage meat
1 beaten egg
1¼ tablespoons milk
3 tablespoons quick cooking rolled oats

For glazing:
¼ tablespoon brown sugar
3 teaspoons flour
¼ teaspoon mustard powder
3 cloves
2 tablespoons fruit juice (canned)
¼ tablespoon vinegar
1¼ tablespoons lemon or orange juice

Mix sausage meat, rolled oats, egg and milk. Chill. Make approximately 32 balls and bake in a shallow dish (325–350°F. — Gas Mark 3) for 30 minutes. Drain off fat. Combine ingredients for glazing. Cook for a few minutes or until slightly thickened. Dip the balls in the glazing. Fix on to cocktail sticks and allow to drain.

1056 MINIATURE PANCAKES

Fill tiny pancakes with creamed chicken or fish. Keep hot until ready to serve. Garnish with peeled shrimps.

1057 SAUSAGE ROLLS

6 oz. flaky pastry
8 oz. sausage meat
egg yolk or milk to glaze

Roll pastry into a long strip. Form the meat into a long roll and place down one side of the pastry. Fold over and seal edges. Make slits across the top and cut into tiny rolls. Brush with milk or egg yolk and bake in a very hot oven (475°F. — Gas Mark 8) for 15–20 minutes.

1058 HOT BACON COCKTAIL SNACKS

Prepare these earlier in the day — pop into the oven as your guests arrive if you have no means of keeping them hot. Cook for 15 minutes in moderately hot oven, or 25 minutes if covered by foil. If you have a hotplate then just transfer them, when cooked, to a serving dish with absorbent kitchen paper underneath so you can prevent their being greasy, and keep on the hotplate so that guests can help themselves. Put firm cocktail sticks through centre of each roll. These snacks can be grilled or fried instead of being cooked in the oven.

1059 Bacon Frankfurters

Wrap small pieces of streaky bacon round cocktail Frankfurter sausages or portions of large sausages. For variety insert fingers of cheese or a small piece of crisp celery in the Frankfurter sausages.

1060 Cheddar Fingers

Wrap small pieces of bacon round fingers of Cheddar cheese, making certain the cheese is completely covered so that it is easy to eat.

1061 DEVILS ON HORSEBACK

Wrap small pieces of bacon round cooked prunes. If wished put a small piece of liver pâté in the centre of each prune.

1062 ANGELS ON HORSEBACK

Wrap small pieces of bacon round well seasoned oysters.

1063 JAFFA ROLLS

Wrap small pieces of bacon round segments of Jaffa oranges. Brush with little butter before cooking.

Colourful cover of George Bernard Shaw's housekeeper's cookbook

1974

GEORGE BERNARD SHAW'S VEGETARIAN COOKBOOK

CHEESE AND CELERY PIE

·

AVOCADO AND ORANGE SALAD

·

QUEEN OF PUDDINGS

MUCH-LAUDED PLAYWRIGHT GEORGE Bernard Shaw was a staunch vegetarian from the age of 25 until he died aged 94. Unsurprisingly, he provided a poetic explanation for his dietary choice, saying Percy Shelley 'opened my eyes to the savagery of my diet' through his poem 'The Revolt of Islam': 'Never again may blood of bird or beast, stain with its venomous stream a human feast'. However, it was suggested in the posthumously published cookbook of his housekeeper, Alice Laden, that it was perhaps born more of necessity. As a young writer, he was almost penniless, living with his mother and walking to the British Museum every day to write, and small vegetarian restaurants down side streets provided good-value sustenance. Regardless of the root cause, it seems that his only 'vice' – for he was also teetotal – was sugar, which, according to Laden, he often 'stuffed into his mouth by the spoonful'. Herself the widow of a strict vegetarian, Laden spent years training in the art of meat-free cooking before happening upon the household as a nurse to Shaw's wife in her final months. So fond was Shaw of Laden's cooking that he convinced her to stay until his death eight years later. With the master of the house banned from the kitchen and menu planning, Alice created something different everyday. Even during the rationing years, Shaw never spared a penny on exotic fruits and vegetables. So he enjoyed everything from gratins and pastries to curries and stews, over three courses at lunch and two at dinner. Those of note include cheese and celery pie; tomato scallops; rice and lentil cutlets; avocado and orange salad; Queen of Puddings; and lemon water ice, with wedges of honey-sweetened cake between meals.

DESSERTS

DESSERTS ARE A CELEBRATION of frivolity, creativity and indulgence. And the menus in this section reflect just that – it is filled with famously outrageous feasts, decadent last meals, and dishes that inspired some of the most renowned artists, writers and musicians of the last two centuries. In the previous chapters, we have seen how food can be trailblazing and a marker for social change. Here, food's function is to entertain, honour or entice, from a cheesy celebration at the White House in 1837 and Oscar Wilde and Arthur Conan Doyle's decadent dinners at The Langham hotel, to Elvis and Priscilla Presley's wedding breakfast and French President François Mitterrand's bizarre final dinner request.

A menu from the last Russian Tsar's coronation

FAMOUS FEASTS

Revelry and feasting are natural bedfellows, and acts of indulgence and grandeur, more often than not, are best showcased by food and drink. The following menus range from Charles Darwin's Oxbridge extravagances to the Deep South wedding breakfast of 'The King'— each as outrageous as the other.

1755   **George II's Christmas Menu**

1804   **Carême's Regency Dinner**

1828   **Charles Darwin's Glutton Club**

1837   **Andrew Jackson's Block of Cheese Party**

1870   **The Paris Siege Christmas Feast**

1896   **The Extravagances of the Last-Ever Tsar**

1967   **Elvis and Priscilla's Wedding Breakfast**

Bill of Fare for
His Majesty's Dinner on Christmass Day, 1755.

First Course.

Top Dish.

The House of a Bird with the Life and Death of a Calf, season'd with Lord Mayor's Pride and Watchman's Delight, and garnish'd with an Old Woman of ninety odd. This was a Soup.

The Remove.

The fleetest Conveyance.

Staves broil'd with Lawyers Fees for Sauce; garnish'd with Horses.

Bottom Dishes.

Fragments of the preserver of Rome in a Pye.

The Sign of the going out of March divided with the Debtors Security, Smart Wine, and the produce of a Walking Stick.

Side Dishes.

Eternal Pikes broil'd.

The Impostors Earwig ragou'd.

Second Course.

Furrows roasted.

An unruly Member chopt small & mixd with reason, and confin'd in a Courtiers promises.

The Top of Corn roasted.

These were the Top, bottom, & middle Dishes.

Side Dishes.

Colour'd Boards fricaseed with Stationer's Ware.

The best of a Foot burnt.

A Ragou of Tops, with the Original of Eternal Pikes, and the Sweet Support of Life cut small.

A British Library Archive copy of George II's Christmas menu, 1755

1755

GEORGE II'S CHRISTMAS MENU

MELANCHOLY SOUP

·

THE DIVINE PART OF A MAN BOILED

·

THE FIRST TEMPATION IN A SMALL BLAST OF WIND

MANY BELIEVE THAT CHRISTMAS TRADITIONS began with Charles Dickens. While it's true that *A Christmas Carol* has a lot to answer for, and that Dickens and his Victorian counterparts were the forerunners for customs that have now become emblematic – such as trees in the living room and crackers to pull on the dining table – the tradition of Christmas dinner was in existence long before then. But in fact, it wasn't just the food: the ubiquitous festive jokes and puzzles can be traced back to King George II's yuletide feasts, although we can't blame this eighteenth century monarch for the paper hats – that was the innovation of a cracker maker in the early 1900s.

According to British Library archival material, the king and his guests were presented with a riddle of a meal – presumably humorous in nature – to figure out while waiting for the first courses. Dishes on this mind-bending Christmas Day menu included 'The House of a Bird ... Garnished with an Old Woman of Ninety', purportedly a soup; 'Fragments of the Preserve of Rome in a Pye'; 'The Impostor's Earring Ragou'd'; 'An Unruly Member Chop't Small and Mix'd with Reason, and Confin'd in a Courtier's Promise', with a side of 'The Bash of the Jest Burnt'. But the fun didn't end there – Boxing Day also appeared to be heavy on the puzzles, including dishes such as 'The Inside of a Snuff Box Roasted', 'Three Dragons Swimming in Cows Blood and Indian Powder', and 'A Plate of Oxford Scholars' for dessert. While Christmas menus have made some advancement in the last 250 years, perhaps the quality of jokes have not.

LE MAITRE D'HOTEL FRANÇAIS.

TABLE DE S. A. R. LE PRINCE RÉGENT,

Servie au pavillon de Brighton, Angleterre, 16 Janvier 1817. Menu de 36 entrées.

HUIT POTAGES.

Le potage à la Condé,
Les nouilles à la Napolitaine,
La julienne au blond de veau,
La bisque d'écrevisses au blanc de volaille,

Le potage de santé, consommé de volaille;
Le potage de perdrix au chasseur,
Le potage à la Hollandaise,
L'orge perlée à la Russe.

HUIT RELEVÉS DE POISSONS.

La hure d'esturgeon au vin de Champagne,
Le gros brochet à la Chambord moderne,
Le turbot à la Hollandaise,
Les tronçons d'anguilles à l'italienne,

Les perches à la Vaterfisch,
Le saumon à la Vénitienne,
Les soles à l'Anglaise, sauce aux huîtres,
Le cabillaud à l'Anglaise, sauce aux homards.

QUATRE GROSSES PIÈCES.

Le dinde aux truffes à la Périgord,
La pièce de bœuf à la cuillère,

Le quartier de veau à la Monglas,
Les faisans à la moderne.

TRENTE-SIX ENTRÉES, DONT QUATRE POUR LES CONTRE-FLANCS.

1. Les escalopes de perdreaux à la Périgord,
2. Les côtelettes de porc frais à la sauce Robert,
3*. Les petits vols-au-vent à la reine,
4. Le fritot de poulets à la tomate,
5. L'émincé de gibier garni de croûtons farcis.

LE GROS BROCHET À LA CHAMBORD.

6. Les filets de gélinottes au chasseur,
7**. La côte de bœuf à la gelée,
8. Les quenelles de volaille à l'Italienne,
9. Le sauté de pigeons à la Toulouse.

LE TURBOT À LA HOLLANDAISE.

10. Les escalopes de ris d'agneaux aux fines herbes,
11. Les filets de moutons à la Conti,
12**. La salade de homards aux laitues,
13. Le sauté de poulardes aux pointes d'asperges.

LES TRONÇONS D'ANGUILLES À L'ITALIENNE.

14. Les filets de faisans à la Pompadour,
15. Les poulets dépecés à la Vénitienne,
16*. Le pâté de lapereaux à l'ancienne,
17. Les papillotes de mauviettes à la Duxelle,
18. Les filets de volaille en damier.

18. Les filets de poulardes à la Chevalier,
17. Les côtelettes de veau à la Polonaise,
16*. La croustade de cailles au gratin,
15. Les ailerons de poulardes à la Macédoine,
14. Le hachis de faisans garni d'œufs pochés.

LES PERCHES A LA WATERFISCH.

13. Les filets de poulardes soufflés au suprême,
12**. Le pain de levrauts à la pelée,
11. Les caisses de foies gras à la Monglas,
10. La fricassée de poulets aux champignons.

LE SAUMON À LA VÉNITIENNE.

9. Le turban de palais de bœufs aux truffes,
8. Les boudins de perdreaux à la Richelieu,
7**. La blanquette de volaille à la magnonaise,
6. Les bécasses à la financière, entrée de broche.

LES SOLES À L'ANGLAISE.

5. Les filets de lapereaux en lorgnettes,
4*. Les côtelettes de mouton glacés, purée de navets;
3. Les petits pâtés à la Russe,
2. Les petits canetons de poulets à la Macédoine,
1. Les aiguillettes de canards à l'orange.

POUR EXTRA, DIX ASSIETTES VOLANTES DE FRITURE.

4. De laitances de carpes à la Harly,
4. De filets mignons panés à l'Anglaise,

2. De filets de perdreaux.

HUIT GROSSES PIÈCES D'ENTREMETS.

Le casque à la Romaine,
Le trophée de marine,
La dinde en galantine sur un socle,
La pyramide de p. de terre à la gelée, à l'Anglaise;

Le palmier aux boucliers,
Le casque à la grecque,
Le signe de saindoux dans une île,
Le jambon gelé sur un socle.

QUATRE PLATS DE ROTS.

Les faisans piqués,
Les poulets à la reine,

Les poulardes à l'Anglaise, sauce aux œufs;
Les gélinottes bardées.

TRENTE-DEUX ENTREMETS.

1. Les champignons grillés, demi-glace;
2**. La gelée de marasquins fouettée,
3. Les pommes de terre frites à la Lyonnaise.

LA GALANTINE SUR UN SOCLE.

4. Les truffes à l'Italienne,
5*. Les gâteaux glacés à la crème au café.

LES FAISANS PIQUÉS.

6*. Les madelaines au cédrat confies,
7**. La gelée de champignons rosée,
8. Les œufs pochés à la chicorée.

LE CASQUE ROMAIN.

9. Les salsifis à la Magnonaise,
10**. La gelée d'orange à la belle vue,
11*. Les marrons d'abricots glacés.

LES POULETS À LA REINE.

12*. Les diadèmes au gros sucre,
13. Les truffes à la serviette.

LA PIRAMYDE DE POMMES DE TERRE À LA GELÉE.

14. Le céleri à la Française,
15**. Le blanc-manger aux noix,
16. Les scakls ou choux de mer au beurre.

16. Les cardes à l'Espagnole,
15**. La crème au caramel, au bain-marie;
14. Les truffes au vin de Champagne.

LE CYGNE DE SAINDOUX DANS UNE ÎLE.

13. Les épinards à l'essence et en croustade,
12*. Les gaufres à la Parisienne.

LES CHAPONS À L'ANGLAISE.

11*. Les choux à la crème de vanille,
10**. La gelée d'ananas garnie,
9. La salade à l'Italienne.

LE CASQUE À LA GRECQUE.

8. Les œufs à l'aurore,
7**. La gelée d'épines-vinettes moulée,
6*. Les fanchonnettes à l'orange.

LES GÉLINOTTES.

5*. Les gâteaux renversés garnis de groseille,
4. Les navets à la Béchamel.

LE JAMBON SUR UN SOCLE.

3. Les truffes à la Périgueux,
2. Le fromage bavarois aux framboises,
1. Les laitues à l'essence de jambon.

POUR EXTRA, SIX ASSIETTES VOLANTES.

Les soufflés en croustade à l'orange, au cédrat, au marasquin, aux avelines.

Carême's Regency dinner menu, 1817

1817

CARÊME'S REGENCY DINNER

IT IS NO EXAGGERATION to say that Marie-Antoine Carême was a godfather of French cooking. Regarded as the antecedent to celebrity chef culture, he worked his way up from kitchen porter to personal chef of the future king of England, George IV, training in patisserie under Sylvain Bailly, a highly acclaimed Parisian pastry chef. After his apprenticeship, Carême set up his own shop, Pâtisserie de la rue de la Paix, and began to carve his formidable reputation for *pièces montées* – enormous confectionery displays of marzipan, sugar, nougat, fondant icing and cake that would be displayed in the windows of stylish shops and at the parties of his wealthy Parisian client base, including one Napoleon Bonaparte. As a consequence of his association with the French leader, he transferred his skills to savoury cooking and became the personal chef of French diplomat Charles Maurice de Talleyrand-Périgord, who challenged him to create a year's worth of seasonal menus, devoid of repetition, with the reward of completing his training as a chef in Talleyrand-Périgord's kitchens; some of these dishes are still at the core of the simple yet chic cooking style that France is known for. After this post, he travelled to Russia, Austria, and England, where he became chef for the Prince Regent, George IV, who had by this stage cultivated a reputation for his love of fine dining, and apparently sampled Carême's food on a state visit to Vienna.

This menu, taken from a dinner hosted by the Prince Regent at the Brighton Pavilion, showcases Carême's signature style: Venetian salmon, turbot with Hollandaise and Italian-style salad, along with his significant flair for presentation. The reason for Carême's departure after eight months remains a little unclear, however, his dislike of the climate and the cuisine are often cited as the culprits.

The Prince Regent's dining room at the Royal Pavilion, Brighton

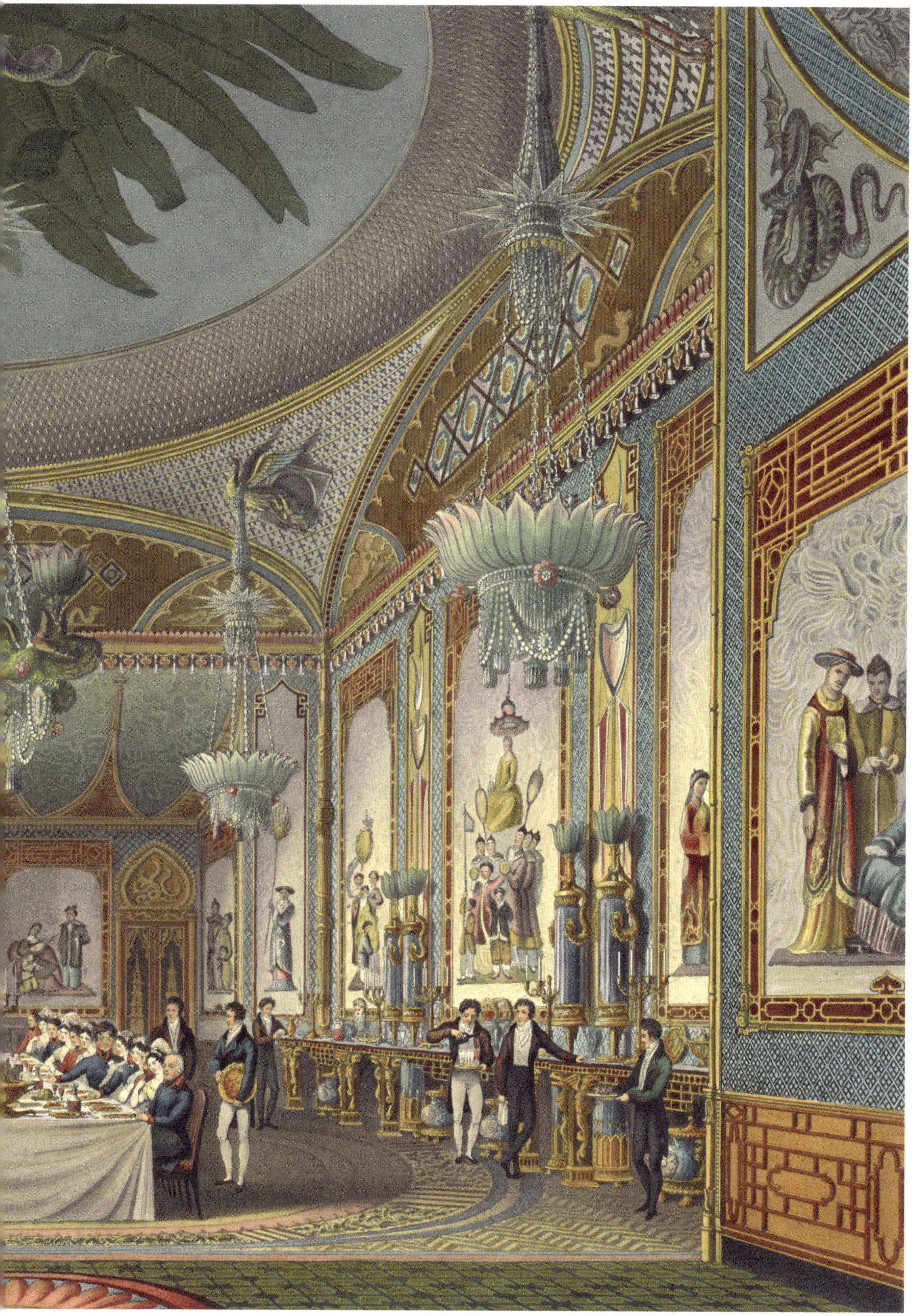

Drawing of a puma from *The Voyage of the Beagle*, 1839

Drawing of a Galápagos marine iguana from *The Voyage of the Beagle*, 1839

1828

CHARLES DARWIN'S GLUTTON CLUB

HAWK

·

BITTERN

·

BROWN OWL

DARWIN, OF COURSE, IS BEST known for this theories on evolution, but another facet to his personality has also been documented – that of his love of food.

In 1828, he had abandoned his medical degree in Edinburgh and instead undertook a degree in theology at the University of Cambridge, with the aim of becoming a clergyman upon graduation. Given his subsequent achievements, it's not a stretch to surmise that he may have started a university society reflecting his interest in nature – and you would be right, but perhaps not quite in the way you might think.

Darwin and his peers established the 'Glutton Club', whose sole purpose was to consume meat that was either unfamiliar or yet to be explored. Reportedly, this included a hawk, a heron-like bird called a bittern, and a particularly unpleasant-tasting brown owl. The latter was, according to reports, the final nail in the coffin for the adventurous club. As a student, his options were limited, but it's a passion that continued into his later life; he ate everything from iguanas in the Galápagos Islands to armadillo and puma. His most famous meal was a nine-kilogram rodent called an agouti, which he declared the 'best meat I ever tasted'.

Jackson's admirers thought that every honor which Jefferson had ever received should be paid him, so some of them, residing in a rural district of New York, got up, under the superintendence of a Mr. Meacham, a mammoth cheese for "Old Hickory." After having been exhibited at New York, Philadelphia, and Baltimore, it was kept for some time in the vestibule at the

THE GREAT CHEESE LEVEE.

White House, and was finally cut at an afternoon reception on the 22d of February, 1837. For hours did a crowd of men, women, and boys hack at the cheese, many taking large hunks of it away with them. When they commenced, the cheese weighed one thousand four hundred pounds, and only a small piece was saved for the President's use. The air was redolent with cheese, the carpet was slippery with cheese, and nothing else

1837

ANDREW JACKSON'S BLOCK OF CHEESE PARTY

NEW YORK STATE AGED CHEDDAR
·
WHISKEY

WHILE THIS MAY SOUND a bit of a unlikely story, the origins of Barack Obama's 'Big Block of Cheese Day' – a moment in which people could interact online with senior presidential staff, seeking answers to any question they'd like to ask the government – actually date back to an event hosted by former US President Andrew Jackson in 1837.

Two years prior to the end of his second term, Jackson was gifted an enormous cheese – weighing in at 660 kilograms (1,400 pounds) – by farmer Thomas S. Meecham of Oswego, a rural area in New York state. Purportedly a case of one-upmanship on the farmer's behalf – a cheese weighing (340 kilograms) 750 pounds had been gifted to Thomas Jefferson by a Massachusetts farmer in 1802 – Jackson had given away as much as he could to friends and advisors before deciding to serve the cheese at his final reception to the general public. According to records, this amounted to around 10,000 people, and while the cheese was swiftly taken care of, the smell, apparently, continued to linger well into successor Martin Van Buren's presidency.

Jackson's cheese party was also immortalised in the American TV series *The West Wing*, which first aired in 1999. Cheddar, it seems, cemented his reputation as a man of the people.

An illustration of the shooting of zoo animals during the Paris Siege

1870

THE PARIS SIEGE CHRISTMAS FEAST

STUFFED DONKEY'S HEAD WITH RADISHES AND BUTTER

BEAN SOUP WITH ELEPHANT BROTH

KANGAROO STEW

WOLF WITH DEER SAUCE

THE FRANCO-PRUSSIAN WAR lasted just six months from July 1870 to January 1871. It saw Paris under siege, resulting in the toppling of Emperor Napoleon III; the expansion of the German Empire; and the rise of a socialist government in the city, known as the Paris commune. The Prussian Army blocked all roads and railways leading to the capital in an attempt to force surrender by cutting off food supplies. But, to the surprise of their enemies, the Parisians did not give up without some serious ingenuity and sacrifice. The city's residents, quite literally, ate every animal available.

Officially cut off on 18 September, citizens continued to eat beef, lamb, pork and fish for the first two months, but by October, horse was on the menu. A month later, in November, these 'household meats' had been rationed to 100 grams per day, and soon, the people were eating rats, cats and dogs.

However desperate times were for most, there was one feast on the ninety-ninth day of the siege – as it happens, Christmas Day – where meat was in abundance, most likely to the detriment of the city zoo. Voisin restaurant served patrons a six-course menu that included the likes of stuffed donkey's head with radishes and butter; bean soup with elephant broth; kangaroo stew; and wolf served with deer sauce. A month later, the city fell to the Prussian Army, with not a trace of the animal kingdom to be seen.

An illustration of the Paris Siege, with butchers selling dogs and cats tibles un étalage de viandes insolites (Voir page 150.)

Москва 18?? 19 мая

Обѣдъ.

Супъ изъ черепахи.

Пирожки.

Рыба Соль. Раковый соусъ.

Филе говядина съ кореньями.

Холодное изъ рябчиковъ и гусиной печенки.

Жаркое: индѣйки и молодые цыплята.

Салатъ.

Цвѣтная капуста и стручки.

Горячій ананасъ съ фруктами.

Мороженое.

Десертъ.

A menu from one of the Tsar's celebration meals

1896

THE EXTRAVAGANCES OF THE LAST-EVER TSAR

BORSCHT

PIROSHKI DUMPLINGS FILLED WITH MEAT

STEAMED FISH

SPRING LAMB

ICE CREAM

AS THE LAST-EVER DYNASTY to rule Russia before the February Revolution of 1917, the Romanov family – and their excesses – have been much documented. From the elaborate costumes of the two-day balls held at the Winter Palace in St Petersburg, to the banquets so elaborate that food was prepared in a building adjacent to the palace (for which a tunnel was created in 1902 to ferry the multi-course meals back and forth in a more effective manner), attention to detail was first and foremost. While it has been said that despite his eccentricities, Tsar Nicholas II was not a particularly fussy eater, a menu from his coronation on 26 May 1896 suggests that certainly the table – and the menu itself – had to look the part.

This menu, designed by artist Viktor Vasnetsov, who was known for his role in the Russian Revivalist movement of the late nineteenth century, indicates that the newly appointed Tsar feasted on classic borscht; steamed fish; spring lamb; piroshki dumplings filled with meat, and ice cream for afters. The coronation dinner took place the day after the event. The Tsar also provided simple food for the people of Moscow to join the palace in the festivities. However, this ended in tragedy, with a stampede that was said to kill around 3,000 people – an event that marked the beginning of the end for the Romanov's 300-year reign.

Left and right: illustrations of the coronation celebration

Народный праздникъ
по случаю Священнаго Коронованія
ИХЪ ВЕЛИЧЕСТВЪ

Elvis and Priscilla Presley cutting their wedding cake, 1967

1967

ELVIS AND PRISCILLA'S WEDDING BREAKFAST

OYSTERS ROCKEFELLER

·

SUCKLING PIG

·

FRIED CHICKEN

·

CHAMPAGNE

·

WEDDING CAKE

MEETING IN 1959 IN WEST Germany, Elvis Presley and Priscilla Beaulieu had a surprisingly long courtship – eight years in fact, before 'The King' proposed in December 1966 at his Graceland home. The couple kept everything a secret until after the ceremony in Las Vegas, when press photographers were invited to come along before the new Mr and Mrs Presley hosted a wedding breakfast for 100 close friends and family members. The most recognised image from the event is that of the newlyweds cutting the six-tier cake, which was five feet tall, flavoured with apricot marmalade, Bavarian cream and kirsch-spiked icing, and covered with fondant flowers, lattice, wedding bells and silver leaves. But the cake was less of a show pony and more of a precedent – their meal, reportedly costing in the region of $10,000 (roughly $80,000 in today's money), was served buffet style, and was a mixture of extravagance and comforting all-American classics: roast suckling pig, oysters Rockefeller, lobster and fried chicken, all served with Champagne. However, Elvis's most famous food association is perhaps the peanut butter, bacon and banana sandwich, the so-called 'Fool's Gold Loaf' – a hollowed-out loaf of bread filled with peanut butter, jam and yes, bacon. With elegance as the order of the day, it's easy to understand why this was off the menu at the nuptials.

A menu from an infamous Savage Club dinner, 1902

FOOD IN THE ARTS

Some of the world's most revered artists, musicians and writers have, it seems, not built their reputation on their creative outlets alone. If you have ever wondered what a famous jazz musician eats after a show, or what the dining preferences of the literary elite are, then look no further.

1801	**The Beginning of Burns Night**
1883	**Savage Club Ball at the Royal Albert Hall**
1889	**Dining at The Langham with Oscar Wilde and Arthur Conan Doyle**
1899	**Picasso's Barcelona Haunt**
1914	**When Poets Ate Peacocks for Dinner**
1920	**Ernest Hemingway's Pan-fried Trout and Pancakes**
1944	**Duke Ellington and His 32 Hotdogs**
1953	**J. D. Salinger's Saturday Roast**
1965	**Ian Fleming: Mission Scott's**
1972	**Surrealist Dinner Party**

Portrait of Burns and his birth place

1801

THE BEGINNING OF BURNS NIGHT

HAGGIS

·

NEEPS AND TATTIES

·

SHEEPS' HEAD

THE SCOTTISH TRADITION OF BURNS Night is celebrated across the globe on 25 January every year, but not many know that the very first supper was held in the middle of summer – 21 July, the anniversary of poet Robert Burns' death, in whose memory the event was created.

While Burns suppers can vary in length and formality, there are three things that are constants – the haggis, the poem recited to it, and whisky. At this inaugural dinner, held in Alloway, Ayrshire, Scotland, nine of the bard's closest friends gathered to pay homage to the man and his work. According to legend, the event was so convivial that they decided to make it an annual event, eventually moving the celebration to Burns' birthday in January.

SAVAGES AT THE ALBERT HALL

THE BUFFALO DANCE AT THE ALBERT HALL
(From "The Graphic")

To face page 232

Illustration of 'The Savages' doing the Buffalo Dance at the Savage Club Ball, Royal Albert Hall
Overleaf: Menu from the Savage Club House Dinner 28 April 1906, drawn by Lawson Wood

1883

SAVAGE CLUB BALL AT THE ROYAL ALBERT HALL

CHAMPAGNE
·
SHERRY
·
COGNAC
·
BLACK COFFEE

ONE OF THE MOST RENOWNED private gentlemen's clubs in the UK, the Savage Club is a collection of literary figures, artists and musicians that was established in London in 1857 as a more bohemian alternative to the pre-existing Garrick Club.

Named after poet Richard Savage, who was the subject of Samuel Johnson's work *The Life of Savage*, the club, which still runs to this day, had famous members such as Mark Twain, J. M. Barrie, W. Somerset Maugham and Dylan Thomas. In addition to the club's prominence in fine arts, it was also the organiser of the first-ever ball at the Royal Albert Hall in July 1883, 12 years after the hall's opening in March 1871. The aim of the ball was to secure more funding for the Royal College of Music. Guests, including the Prince and Princess of Wales, were served food and drinks – which we know at the very least consisted of sherry, cognac, black coffee and Champagne. This was followed by a late-night performance of the Buffalo Dance, a tradition exercised by the Native American communities of North America. Members of the club were the stars, dressed in costumes imitating traditional dress. The Savage Club was known for hosting notable and somewhat eccentric dinners, always followed by entertainment – with elaborately illustrated menu cards to match.

SAVAGE

APRIL 22

H. GREVILLE

MENU

SOUPS
Jardinier
Mock Turtle

· FISH ·
Salmon Tartare Sauce
Cucumber

· ENTREE ·
Sweetbreads
a 'la Macedoine

· JOINT ·
Fore Qr of Lamb
Mint Sauce

· SWEETS ·
Rhubarb Tart
Vanilla Creams

Parmesan Straws
Biscuits

THE BAR

"Gentlemen, you may smoke!"

Lawson Wood

CLUB · HOUSE DINNER ·
·6
GOMERY M.P.
THE CHAIR ·
THE FIRST SAVAGE CLUB DINNER ·
SAVAGE CLUB 15 MILES
"BEHIND TIME"
E IN ?"

'The Cipher and the Man Who Solved It', an illustration from *The Valley of Fear*, *The Strand Magazine*, September 1914

1889

DINING AT THE LANGHAM WITH OSCAR WILDE AND ARTHUR CONAN DOYLE

VENETIAN-STYLE FILLET OF SOLE

·

RIB OF BEEF WITH YORKSHIRE PUDDING

·

POTATO GRATIN

·

PISTACHIO ICE CREAM

THE LANGHAM IN MARYLEBONE, London, has been graced with many a distinguished guest, and was the first of Europe's 'grand' hotels; so grand, in fact, that the Prince of Wales attended its opening party in 1865. What qualified it as such was its innovative features that embraced industrial advancements like hydraulic lifts, electric lights and water closets, along with its luxurious fittings – not to mention famous guests. Indeed, Napoleon III resided at The Langham during the siege of Paris in 1870, and it was a favourite of Charles Dickens, Mark Twain, Noël Coward and Wallis Simpson. Perhaps, though, its most famous fan was Sir Arthur Conan Doyle, creator of Sherlock Holmes, who even set parts of A Scandal in Bohemia and The Sign of Four at the hotel. The story behind the latter, however, has a twist.

In the summer of 1889, Conan Doyle dined with publishing agent J. M. Stoddart to discuss contributing to *Lippincott's Monthly Magazine*, and they were joined by another guest – Oscar Wilde. Over dinner, the men agreed to each write a short story for Stoddart, which turned into Conan Doyle's *The Sign of Four*, and arguably Wilde's most impactful work, *The Picture of Dorian Gray*. While there's no official record of what the men ate, we do know what was on the menu at the time: Venetian-style fillet of sole, rib of beef with Yorkshire pudding, potato gratin, a selection of cheeses, and pistachio ice cream. In 2010, a green plaque was placed on the wall outside the restaurant to commemorate the occasion, and in 2014, their dinner menu was replicated by The Langham in celebration of this significant event.

Menu from Els Quatre Gats drawn by Pablo Picasso, 1899

1899

PICASSO'S BARCELONA HAUNT

TORTILLA WITH AIOLI
·
CATALAN SAUSAGE AND BEANS

PABLO PICASSO WAS FAMOUSLY a man who appreciated good food – his depiction of all things edible became a touring exhibition in Europe in 2018, with the likes of Spanish chef Ferran Adrià paying homage to both the artist's work and his appetite. But where did it all start? Perhaps, it could be argued, at Els Quatre Gats in Barcelona's infamous gothic quarter. The restaurant became a hangout for artists in the emerging Modernist movement, and Picasso, aged 17, joined the crowds nightly when he moved to the city. With a bar and cabaret performances in the back room, Els Quatre Gats was lively, bohemian and so loved by Picasso that he even held his first solo exhibition of 25 charcoal and watercolour works in the restaurant – and illustrated the menus.

Reportedly, Picasso was a man of simple tastes when it came to dinner, preferring unfussy, seasonal and local food to anything with too many flourishes. To that end, when discussing his and his first wife's tastes, he said, 'Olga loves cakes and caviar, I love Catalan sausage and beans'. On many occasions after a dinner such as this, the young artist would auction his sketches, and while his fortunes improved in later life, his culinary tastes remained humble. In a *Vogue* interview in 1964, he declared that his favourite meal of all time was Spanish tortilla served with aioli.

The poets gathered outside Blunt's house, 1914

1914

WHEN POETS ATE PEACOCKS FOR DINNER

ROASTED BEEF

·

ROAST PEACOCK

IN A SEMINAL MEETING between men of the arts, poets Ezra Pound, W. B. Yeats, and the less-well-remembered Victor Plarr, Thomas Sturge Moore, Richard Aldington and Frank Flint gathered at the house of Wilfrid Scawen Blunt in rural Sussex. However, instead of breaking bread, they roasted peacock. The meeting was at the request of Ezra Pound, who made it his aim to meet every poet in England while he was living with Yeats and working as his secretary. Blunt, himself a poet, was the husband of the late Lord Byron's granddaughter, Lady Anne Isabella Noel Byron. At the request of Lady Gregory, Yeats' close friend and patron, the bird was served alongside its signature plumage, preceded by a much tamer main course of roast beef.

After the meal, the men posed for a photograph – an image that hit newspapers in England, Ireland and the US shortly afterwards. At the time, Blunt was something of a social impresario, and as part of growing interest in the 'celebrity' of artists, such meetings were widely reported and written about. One such occasion became legend when Ezra Pound reportedly, while having a drink in the London pub Ye Old Cheshire Cheese, ate a bunch of tulips while discussing his work. Nothing has been reported as to whether the group rated the meal, however, as a gift to their host, the poets presented Blunt with a small, hand-carved box made of stone, in which each had placed some of their most recent works.

Hemingway and his catch at Walloon Lake, Michigan, date unknown

1920

ERNEST HEMINGWAY'S PAN-FRIED TROUT AND PANCAKES

PANCAKES WITH APPLE BUTTER AND CINNAMON SUGAR

·

BACON FAT-FRIED TROUT

HEMINGWAY WAS WELL KNOWN for his love of good food – *A Moveable Feast* is often regarded as a city guide like no other, whisking readers through the restaurants and bars of Paris with some of the twentieth century's most lauded artists and writers in tow. In addition, he was a great outdoorsman, as passionate about fly fishing and camping as he was his more urban pursuits. As part of a series of columns written for Canadian newspaper the *Toronto Star Weekly*, he wrote short stories inspired by his camping trips, and in one such article, the young writer extolled the virtues of a week or two spent in the wilds.

The foundation of any good camping holiday, according to Hemingway, was food. His belief was that 'the rock that wrecks most camping trips is cooking'. Offering a detailed recipe as a solution to this common problem, he suggested having a frying pan at the ready to cook pancakes topped with apple butter and cinnamon sugar so that 'the crowd have taken the edge off their appetites' while the trout cooked, using bacon fat to baste it and ensure the fish is well cooked. Finally, he declared, 'if there is anything better than that combination, the writer has yet to taste it in a lifetime devoted largely and studiously to eating'. And if that was the standard of dining on every trip that Hemingway took, who are we to argue?

Duke Ellington on stage in New York, 1946

1944

DUKE ELLINGTON AND HIS 32 HOT DOGS

BLACK TEA
·
SHREDDED WHEAT
·
32 HOT DOGS

AMERICAN COMPOSER AND MUSICIAN Duke Ellington is a legend of the jazz world. A regular performer in the jazz clubs of downtown Manhattan and Harlem in the 1920s and 1930s, Ellington and his band went on to make more than a thousand records between 1927 and 1974, and undisputedly blazed a trail for many a jazz performer to come. But while he will, first and foremost, be remembered for his music, those close to him had recollections of more than just his musical talent – namely, his love of food.

He would order shredded wheat and black tea when on the straight and narrow, but Ellington's appetite was unparalleled, despite his best intentions. In his own words, 'I got the reputation of eating more hot dogs than any man in America. A Mrs Wagner [at Old Orchard Beach Restaurant, Maine] makes a toasted bun that's the best of its kind in America. She has a toasted bun, then a slice of onion, then a hamburger, then a tomato, then melted cheese, than another hamburger, then a slice of onion, more cheese, more tomato, and then the other side of the bun. Her hot dogs have two dogs to a bun. I ate 32 in one night'.

At one of the oldest beach resorts in Maine, Ellington and his orchestra worked up an appetite by frequently playing at the Pier Casino and the Palace in the town, where his meals, as well as his music, will forever be celebrated.

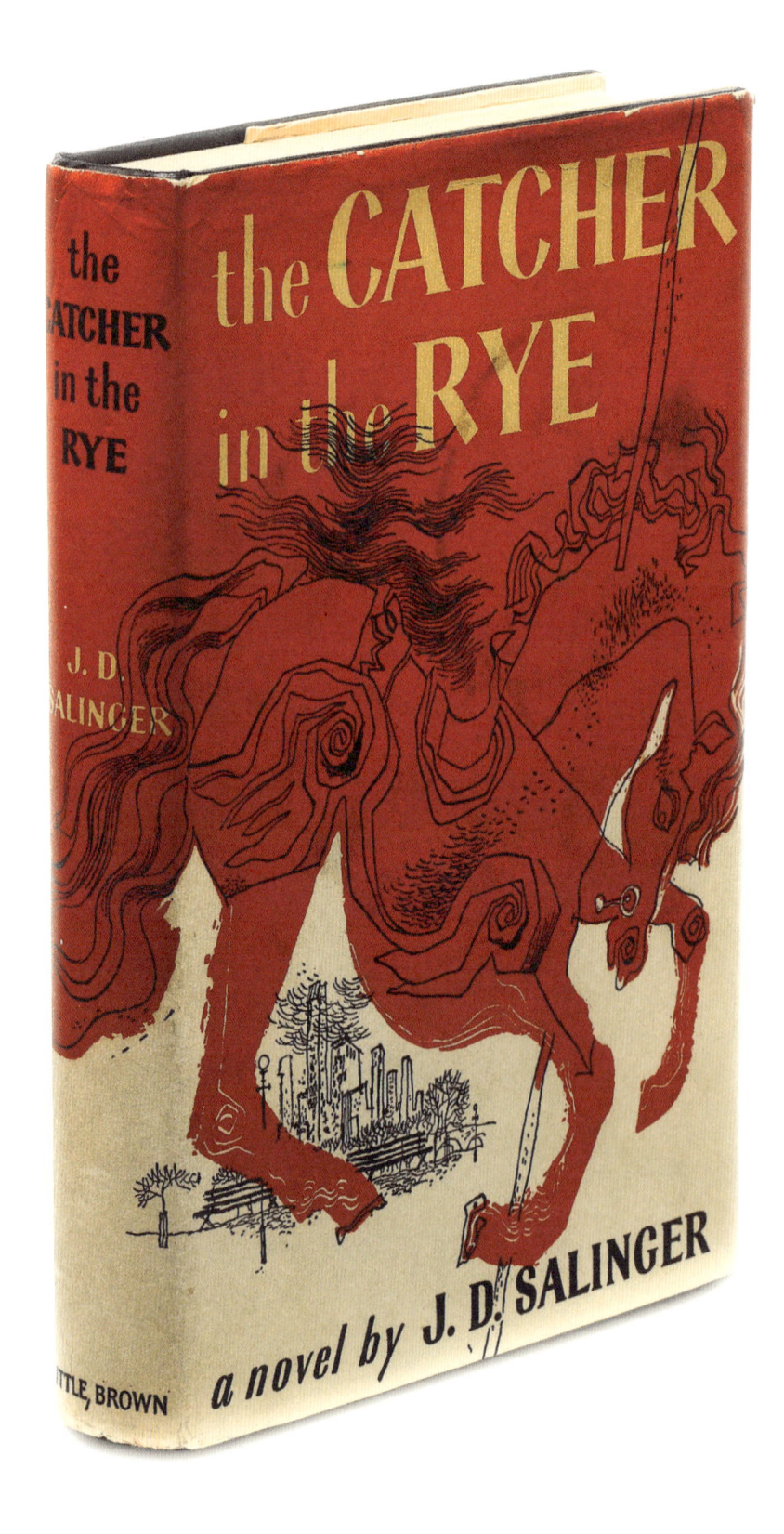

Cover to the first edition of *The Catcher in the Rye*, 1954

1953

J. D. SALINGER'S SATURDAY ROAST

ROAST BEEF

·

SWEET PIES

PUBLISHED IN 1951, *The Catcher in the Rye* is arguably one of the most influential works of the twentieth century, and its author, J. D. Salinger, is almost as well known for his subsequent seclusion in rural New Hampshire as he is for this coming-of-age novel. The novel's protagonist, Holden Caulfield, first appeared as a character in a short story called 'I'm Crazy', published in 1945, but it was his subsequent appearance in *The Catcher in the Rye* that caught the world's attention, and to date, more than 70 million copies of the book have been sold worldwide.

Contrary to a popular and almost mythical belief, Salinger's self-imposed 'exile' from New York literary circles to the town of Cornish, New Hampshire, was actually punctuated with social events. These included the weekly 'Saturday Supper' of roast beef at the Congregational Church of Hartland, Vermont. Salinger always arrived early and sat close to the table of sweet pies served for dessert. The author would purportedly sit quietly and spend the evening writing in his spiral notebook. Unsurprisingly, the diet of his character Holden Caulfield has received much deeper discussion: his commiseration meal of a grilled cheese sandwich and malted milk after a less-than-successful date has been recreated by bloggers, writers and cooks alike.

This picture depicts the site of Scott's Restaurant as it probably looked in the middle of the 17th Century — The Windmill in the background gave the name to Gt. Windmill Street which runs alongside Scott's Restaurant to-day

Scott's

To the Librarian of the Corporation of London Guildhall, the Secretary of the London Society, the Secretary of the London Topographical Society, and the Officials of the British Museum, we express our best thanks for the great assistance given to us in drawing up this cover, including the "Story of Pickadilly" which can be read on the back page.

SCOTT'S RESTAURANT LIMITED
Coventry Street, London, W.1

Scott's menu, 1965

1965

IAN FLEMING: MISSION SCOTT'S

CHAMPAGNE

·

OYSTERS

·

DRY MARTINI

'SHAKEN, NOT STIRRED' IS PERHAPS one of the most famous lines in cinema history, but James Bond's immortal words have their roots in reality – Scott's of Mayfair, to be exact. The famous West London seafood restaurant opened as an oyster shack in the mid-1800s, evolved into a hot spot of the well-to-do in the twentieth century, and became a favourite of author Ian Fleming in the 1950s and 1960s. He frequented Scott's during his time in the intelligence service, and was famously suspected of being a German spy while dining there during the Second World War, when the head waiter heard him speaking in German and reported him to Scotland Yard. In actual fact, he was on a mission, attempting to out a mole. Indeed, his fictional spy was also a fan. The restaurant often featured in Fleming's novels, with the two even sharing a favourite table – right hand corner, first floor, in the window above the street light. In addition to freshly shucked oysters, Champagne and high-quality seafood, the restaurant served dry martinis, just how Fleming – and Bond – liked them. It's also namechecked as a date-night destination in *Moonraker*, as Bond planned to take Mary Goodnight.

WHITE STAR LINE.

R.M.S. "TITANIC."   APRIL 14, 1912.

THIRD CLASS.

BREAKFAST.

Oatmeal Porridge & Milk
Smoked Herrings, Jacket Potatoes
Ham & Eggs
Fresh Bread & Butter
Marmalade   Swedish Bread
Tea   Coffee

DINNER.

Rice Soup
Fresh Bread   Cabin Biscuits
Roast Beef, Brown Gravy
Sweet Corn   Boiled Potatoes
Plum Pudding, Sweet Sauce
Fruit

TEA.

Cold Meat
Cheese   Pickles
Fresh Bread & Butter
Stewed Figs & Rice
Tea

SUPPER.

Gruel   Cabin Biscuits   Cheese

Any complaint respecting the Food supplied, want of attention or incivility, should be at once reported to the Purser or Chief Steward. For purposes of identification, each Steward wears a numbered badge on the arm.

Menu for third-class passengers on *Titanic*, dated the day the ship hit an iceberg

LAST MEALS

A fitting final chapter, these last meals range from the unprecedented to the meticulously planned, and from the humble to the downright bizarre. Whether it's the swan song of a famous restaurant or the last bite of an infamous political figure, the following feasts have marked everything from seismic disasters to turning points in history.

1864	Abraham Lincoln's Last Christmas
1912	Last Meal on the Titanic
1916	Rasputin's Final Mouthful
1965	King Farouk of Egypt's Grand Finale
1974	President Nixon's Last Lunch in the White House
1995	François Mitterrand's Swan Song
2011	El Bulli's Last Service

'The Union Christmas Dinner', an illustration by Thomas Nast in *Harper's Weekly*, 1864

1864

ABRAHAM LINCOLN'S LAST CHRISTMAS

TURKEY

·

EGGNOG

·

FRUIT CAKE

AMONG THE COUNTLESS TALES of culinary extravagance and commitment to indulgence that surround many a world leader comes that of the American President Abraham Lincoln – a man of such simple tastes that breakfast was barely more than a cup of coffee, and even the most luxurious dinner was two courses at best. However, the Christmas of 1864 was significant for two reasons: firstly, it marked the beginning of the end of the American Civil War with the fall of Savannah, Georgia, and secondly, it was to be President Lincoln's last before his assassination on 14 April 1865.

In celebration of General Sherman's victory in the south, Lincoln ordered a 300-gun salute on Christmas Day, and, in keeping with the sudden festive spirit, the president's young son, Tad, invited in a group of local newspaper correspondents, who were tired and hungry from the cold. Turkey was definitely on the menu, along with eggnog, oranges and fruit cake. At the time, Christmas was not yet a state holiday – that came five years later. It's often claimed that Lincoln had very little spirit, but with his term mostly being during the Civil War, his reserved festivities are somewhat understandable.

R.M.S. "TITANIC"
April 14, 1912

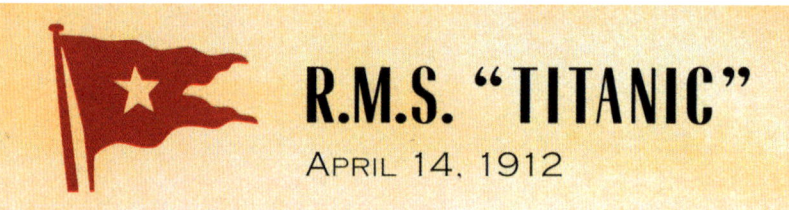

FIRST CLASS DINNER

Hors d'oeuvre Varies

Oysters

Consomme Olga   Cream of Barley

Salmon, Mousseline Sauce, Cucumber

Filet Mignons Lili

Saute of Chicken Lyonnaise

Vegetable Marrow Farcie

Lamb, Mint Sauce

Roast Duckling, Apple Sauce

Sirloin of Beef   Chateau Potatoes

Green Peas   Creamed Carrots

Boiled Rice

Parmentier & Boiled New Potatoes

Punch Romaine

Roast Squab & Cress

Red Burgundy

Cold Asparagus   Vinaigrette

Pate de Foie Gras

Celery

Waldorf Pudding

Peaches in Chartreuse Jelly

Chocolate & Vanilla Eclairs

French Ice Cream

First class menu on board the *Titanic*

1912

LAST MEAL ON THE TITANIC

THE FINAL FEAST OF THE first-class passengers on board RMS *Titanic* is perhaps one of the most legendary meals of the twentieth century. Decadent and joyous, this scene has been captured in countless books and films over the last 100 years. It is said that to sustain the thousands of passengers, from first to third class, there were 19 ovens in the kitchen, a specialised room of cutlery, and even a kind of butcher's shop and greengrocers aboard the ship.

The only menu recovered from the last night of *Titanic*'s voyage was that of the first-class dining room, where guests could eat more than ten courses of an evening, all paired with fine wines. On what was fated to be the final meal served – the ship hit the iceberg just before midnight on 14 April 1912 – the evening kicked off with freshly shucked oysters and was followed by consommé, salmon with mousseline sauce, filet mignon, roast duckling and apple sauce, roast squab, cold asparagus and pâté de foie gras, to name a few, concluding with chocolate eclairs, peaches in jelly, and ice cream.

Of the kitchen staff survivors, perhaps most the most famous tale is that of the head baker, Charles Joughin of Birkenhead, England. Not only did he gather bread for the lifeboats, he gave up his seat on the last lifeboat, and miraculously managed to tread water in the ocean for almost three hours before his rescue.

Portrait of Rasputin, date unknown

1916

RASPUTIN'S FINAL MOUTHFUL

ZAKUSKI

·

FISH SOUP

·

HONEY CAKES

GRIGORI RASPUTIN, SPIRITUAL AIDE to Tsar Nicholas II of Russia, is famous more for the myths that surround his association with the Romanov family than the facts of his actual existence, of which there are few.

Latterly known as the 'mad monk', Rasputin's early life was spent in Siberia, where he was born to poor parents. At the age of 23 – in spite of already having a wife and children – he experienced a spiritual awakening after spending time in a monastery. In the ensuing years, he became acquainted with various religious figures in the Russian Orthodox church, finally meeting with the Romanov family in 1906. By the time of the First World War, Rasputin had become an indispensable spiritual advisor to the Tsar's wife, Alexandra, and a healer to their son, Alexei, and the rest of the story is the stuff of legend.

Much is debated about his tastes when it came to dinner time, and it varies from biographer to biographer as to whether it's believed that he indulged like the aristocracy on Champagne and caviar, or ate the simpler food of his heritage – black bread, root vegetables and tea. However, what all agree on is his love of wine, specifically Madeira, and his terrible table manners – he supposedly licked his fingers while eating and often had food caught in his beard.

On the night of his death, the 'mad monk' reportedly ate *zakuski* (Russian hors d'oeuvres) and fish soup before being lured by his executioner, Felix Yusupov, to eat honey cakes at his home – accompanied, as always, by a lot of Madeira. Whether his food was laced with poison is unclear, but either way, after dinner, he was shot dead and thrown in the Malaya Nevka river. Just two months later, the Romanov dynasty was toppled.

King Farouk with his daughter, Farial

1965

KING FAROUK OF EGYPT'S GRAND FINALE

OYSTERS
·
ROAST LAMB
·
CAKE

KING OF EGYPT FROM the age of 16, Farouk I was a controversial leader to the last. The monarchy, having been created by the British, was a relatively recent creation, and Farouk was the tenth king on the throne. His excesses and indulgences – whisky, wine, good food, and if reports are to be believed, a pornographic necktie collection – led him to be regarded as more of a cad and playboy than a dutiful leader. So it came as no surprise that in 1952, after 16 years in power, the King was overthrown in a coup initiated by the Egyptian Army. Farouk and his family fled to Italy – although his baby son was declared the new king of Egypt – and eventually he settled in Monaco, where he continued to live a life of frivolity until his death in 1965.

As befit his extravagant life, Farouk's death was dramatic. After dining on oysters, roast lamb and cake at Ile de France restaurant in Rome – with a notably younger female companion – the former king suffered a heart attack while smoking a cigar, and died at the scene, aged just 45 years old.

Photograph of Nixon's final lunch in the White House

1974

PRESIDENT NIXON'S LAST LUNCH IN THE WHITE HOUSE

COTTAGE CHEESE WITH PINEAPPLE
·
GLASS OF MILK

RICHARD NIXON'S SECOND TERM in the White House was perhaps one of the most controversial of American history, tainted as it was by the Watergate scandal. In this time, it was discovered that his administration bugged the Democratic National Committee headquarters in Washington D.C., which, among numerous other political indiscretions such as harassment and lying under oath, led to the prosecution of nearly 50 officials. Understandably, this information destabilised the public's trust in Nixon, and to avoid his inevitable removal from office, Nixon chose to resign, live on national television, on 9 August 1974.

Nixon's standard fodder while in office had an all-American-comfort bent – meatloaf, ice cream sundaes – but on the day of his resignation, his lunch order was simple: pineapple, cottage cheese, and a glass of milk. Within 24 hours, Nixon had stepped down, and Vice President Gerald Ford was sworn in. Robert Knudsen, the official White House photographer of the time, although not in the habit of snapping presidential meals, captured the solitary dish. It has now become a poignant depiction of the only time in the history of US government that a president resigned from his post.

Ortolans prepared for eating

1995

FRANÇOIS MITTERAND'S SWAN SONG

OYSTERS
·
FOIE GRAS
·
CAPON
·
ORTOLAN

FRANÇOIS MITTERAND WAS BOTH the first socialist to be elected in France and the longest running president, in office from 1981 to 1995. Prior to his political career, Mitterand was in the French Army during the Second World War, but was captured by the Germans and sent to a prison camp, before escaping and joining the resistance in 1943. In the following years, he rose through the ranks of the Socialist Party, eventually coming to power as leader of the Fifth Republic of France.

While his tenure was inevitably a series of highs and lows, given its length, Mitterand's final feast, served just days before his death from prostate cancer on 8 January 1996, was the epitome of indulgence. Mitterand's meal included oysters, foie gras, a capon, and a native bird known as an ortolan – a small songbird that supposedly symbolises the French soul. And while it was highly prized on the dining table, it was also highly illegal to eat. Traditionally, the bird is eaten under the cover of a white cloth, and put in the mouth in its entirety – head, bones and all – and they are often killed by being drowned in a vat of Armangnac. Quite the way to bow out, for both parties.

Staff prepping at El Bulli

2011

EL BULLI'S FINAL SERVICE

PASSIONFRUIT 'CAVIAR'

·

DES/SERT

·

LOBSTER AND LAMB'S BRAIN SALAD

THE RISE OF MOLECULAR GASTRONOMY in the 1990s and 2000s is often credited, in part, to Spanish chef Ferran Adrià, the man behind El Bulli, an award-winning, innovative restaurant that earned three Michelin stars and made countless 'best of' lists. Located in the northern Catalonian coastal town of Roses, El Bulli was, at first, a beach bar, but from 1961 to 2011, it morphed from simple sustenance to food as artistic expression. Adrià's apprentices include some of the most famous chefs working in the world today: Massimo Bottura of Osteria Francescana, René Redzepi of Noma, Andoni Luis Aduriz of Mugaritz, and Joan Roca of El Celler de Can Roca, to name but four. In its last weeks before closing in 2011, the restaurant hosted final dinners for journalists, elites, and downright food obsessives, celebrating some of the restaurant's most famous dishes, such as the liquid olive created through reverse spherification – arguably one of the most iconic dishes in the canon of molecular gastronomy.

El Bulli's final dinner, The Last Waltz, was attended by the family and friends of the 45 permanent staff working at the time, plus alumni. The meal, which was 50 courses, was mostly kept a secret. However, it was reported that the meal celebrated many of the restaurant's iconic dishes – passionfruit 'caviar', Des/sert, lobster and lamb's brain salad – and ended with Adrià's take on peach Melba, a dish invented by the godfather of nouvelle cuisine, Auguste Escoffier. The last dish was met with rapturous applause, and the party, unsurprisingly, went on until dawn.

INDEX

Page numbers in *italics* refer to photographs, illustrations and captions

Abbott, Edward 141
Abraham, Dr Phineas S. *184*
Acton, Eliza 131, *132*, 133
Adrià, Ferran 195, 221
Aduriz, Andoni Luis 221
Air France *114*, 129
Air Raid Lunch 151, *153*
Albert Hall 185, *188*, 189
Aldington, Richard *196*, 197
Aldrin, Buzz 127
Alexandra, Princess of Wales 189
Alexandra, Tsarina 213
Alexei, Tsarevich 213
Almond, W. Douglas *184*
Alper, Sam 41
American Civil War 209
Ando, Momofuku 57
Apollo 11 127
Armstrong, Neil 127
Army Ordnance Corps 91
Astoria, *see* Waldorf-Astoria
Atlantic, Battle of the 151
Atlee, Clement 99

baked beans 11, *48*, 49, *50–1*
Barrie, J. M. 189
Bartender's Guide (Thomas) 47
'Beanz Meanz Heinz' campaign 49
Beeton, Isabella 137
Beeton's Book of Household Management (Beeton) 19, 81, 131, *136*, 137, *138–9*
Behring, Emil von *88*, 89
Belafonte, Harry 109
Berkeley, NY 121
Bernhardt, Sarah 69
Big Block of Cheese Day 173
black-out taxi service 151
Blackpool Tower 63, *72*, 73
Blighty 82
Blitz 151
Blumenthal, Heston 2, 79
Blunt, Wilfrid Scawen *196*, 197
Bocuse, Paul 129
Bonaparte, Napoleon 167
Boots 59
Bottura, Massimo 221
Bridges, Styles *110*
Brighton Pavilion 167, *168–9*
British Airways (BA) 129
British Library *164*, 165
British Museum 159
Buckingham Palace 84
Buffalo Dance *188*, 189
Burger King 41
Burns Night 185, 187
Burns, Robert *186*, 187
Buttolph Collection 66
Byron, Lady Anne Isabella Noel 197
Byron, Lord 197

Cadbury's Milk Tray *32*, 33
California Railway Dinner (1959) 83, *104*, 105, *106*, 107
Cambridge University 171
Canteen at the Front *116*
Canter, David 77
Carême, Marie-Antoine 69, 163, *166*, 167

Carnaby Street, London 77
carte, defined 6
The Catcher in the Rye (Salinger) *202*, 203
Chaney, Red 53
cheese party (1837) 173
Chinese:
 ready meals 55
 restaurants/takeaways 38, 39, 55
chocolate(s):
 boxes of 17, *32*, 33
 cakes 44, 45
Christmas, Paris Siege (1870) 163, 175
Christmas WWI (1917) 11, *90*, 91, *92*
A Christmas Carol (Dickens) 165
Christmas menu (1755) *164*, 165
Christmas truce (1914) 91, *93*
Christmas Union Dinner (1864) *208*, 209
Chung Koon 39
Churchill, Sir Winston 11, 75, 83, *96*, 97
cinema food 17, *36*, 37
'The Cipher and the Man Who Solved It' (Keller) *192*
cocktails 17, *46*, 47, *47*, 121
Cold War 109
Colonies and Ships Commerce *140*
Commodore, NY *120*, 121
Conan Doyle, Sir Arthur 161, 185, 193
concession stands 36
Concorde *114*, 115, 129
Congregational Church of Hartland 203
cookbooks 11, 19, 131
cooked-from-scratch food 147
Cookery in Colour (Patten) 11, 131, *154*, 155, *156–7*
Corrigan, Richard 129
Coventry Evening Telegraph 31
Coward, Sir Noël 193
Cranks 63, *76*, 77
Crimean War 135
Cuban Missile Crisis (1962) 105
Cubism 143
Cunard-White Star Line 75
Cup Noodle 57
curry houses 16, 17, 23
Curtis, Tony 109

Darwin, Charles 163, 171
Delmonico, Lorenzo 65
Delmonico's *62*, 63, *64–5*, *64–5*, 66
Demel Patisserie 45
Democratic National Committee (DMC) 217
Design Cuisine 113
Diana, Princess of Wales 77
Dickens, Charles 25, 165, 193
Dig for Victory *130*
dining-car service 17, *26*, 28, *29*
'Dinners without Delay for Busy and Business Housekeepers' (Marsh) 147
Disney, Walt 75
Disneyland 105

Dover Express 123
drive-thrus/drive-ins 42, 52, 53, 147
Dunant, Henry *88*, 89

East India Company 23
Education Act (1944) 123
Edward VII 69, 189, 193
Eighteenth Amendment (US) 121
Eisenhower, Dwight D. 105
El Bulli 207, *220*, 221
El Celler de Can Roca 221
Eliot, T. S. 75
Ellington, Duke 185, *200*, 201
Els Quatre Gats *194*, 195
The English and Australian Cookery Book (Abbott) *140*, 141
The Epicurean (Ranhofer) *18*, 19, 67
The Epicure's Almanack (Rylance) 23
Escoffier, Auguste 11, 15, 63, 69, 221
Everybody 24

Farial, Princess *214*
farmers' markets 17, *34*, 35
Farouk I 207, *214*, 215
fast food 15, 17, *40*, 41, 42, 147
The Fat Duck 63, *78*
February Revolution (1917) 179
Fillia 143
First Panel Sheriff's Jury Annual Dinner 66
First World War 11, 35, 81, *82*, 90, 91, *116*, 117, *118–19*, 213
fish and chips 17, *24*, 25
Fitzgerald, Ella 109
Fleming, Ian 185, 205
Flint, Frank *196*, 197
Fool's Gold Loaf 183
Ford, Gerald 217
Foreign Press Association (FPA) 98, *99*, *100–1*
Fortnum & Mason 49
Franco-Prussian War 175
French cuisine 68, 69
full English breakfast, first adopted 49
The Futurist Cook Book (Marinetti) *142*, 143
Futurist food *142*, 143, *144–5*

Galápagos Islands *170*, 171
Garrick Club 189
Gateway of India 103
gelinottes 89
George II 163, *164*, 165
George IV 167, *168–9*
Gettysburg Address 113
GHI (Good Housekeeping Institute) 147
Glutton Club 163, 171
Good Housekeeping Book of Menus (GHI) *146*, 147, *148*, *149*
Graceland 183
The Grand Hotel, Monte Carlo 69
The Grand Hotel, Oslo 89
Grand Hyatt, NY 121
The Graphic *188*
Great Cheese Levee *172*
Great Depression 35, 37

Great Northern Railway (GNR) 27, 28
Gregory, Lady 197
Grill Room, Commodore, NY 120
Guardian, The 113

H. J. Heinz 11, *48*, 49
Halleck, Charles A. *110*
Hamlyn 155
Hampton Court Palace 31
Harper's Weekly 208
haute-style French cuisine 103
Hayden, Carl *110*
Heathrow Airport 129
Heinz Baked Beans ('Heinz Beanz') *48*, 49
Hemingway, Ernest 12, 109, 185, *198*, 199
Hindoostane Coffee House 23
HMSO 124
Hoff, Jacobus H. van 't *88*, 89
Hollywood 105, 109
hospital food 81, 115
Hotel Cecil *13*
Hotel Sacher *44*, 45

ice cream 60, *61*, 65
ice vendors *60*
Ile de France 215
Illustrated London News 27, *93*
Immortal Trout 143
In-N-Out Burger *42*, *52*, 53
Indian:
    ready meals 55
    restaurants/takeaways 16, 17, 23
Indian Independence Day 11
Indian Independence Dinner (1947) 83, 103
instant noodles *56*, 57
International Committee of the Red Cross 89
The Invention of the Restaurant (Spang) 9
Irving, Henry 184
Issoudin, France *118–19*

Jackson, Andrew 163, 173
James Bond 205
Jefferson, Thomas 173
JFK Inauguration Lunch (1961) 83, *108*, 109, *110–11*
John F. Kennedy International Airport 129
Johnson, Lyndon B. *110*
Johnson, Samuel 189
Joughin, Charles 211

Kennedy, John F. *110*
Kennedy, John F. ('JFK') 83, *108*, 109, *110–11*
Khrushchev, Nikita 83, 105, *106*
Khrushcheva, Nina Petrovna 105, *106*
Kitchen Front *150*
Knudsen, Robert 217
Kurakin, Alexander ('Diamond Prince') 19

Laden, Alice *158*, 159
The Langham 161, 185, 193
'The Last Guest' *222*
The Last Waltz 221
Le Guide Culinaire (Escoffier) 69
Lexington Day *116*
The Life of Savage (Johnson) 189
Lincoln, Abraham 113, 207, *208*, 209

Lincoln, Thomas ('Tad') 209
Lippincott's Monthly Magazine 193
Little Chef 17, *40*, 41
Lobster Newberg 64–5
Lotus House 39
Lucas, Charles *29*
Lucky House Takeaway *38*
Lumière brothers 37

McCartney, Linda 77
McCartney, Paul 77
McCormack, John W. *110*
McDonald's 41
Maconchie's meat stew 91
Mahomed, Sake Dean *22*, 23
Maison Prunier 10, 151, *152–3*
Malaya Nevka, River 213
Malin, Joseph 17, 25
Manifesto of Futurist Cooking (Marinetti, Fillia) 143
A Manual of Domestic Economy (Walsh) 20–1
Mao Zedong 39
Marco Polo 61
Marinetti, Filippo Tommaso 143
Marks & Spencer 55, 59
Marsh, Dorothy 147
Martini 15, *46*, 47, *47*
Maugham, W. Somerset 189
Meecham, Thomas S. 173
'Melody and Merriment Ringing in the Trenches' (*The War Illustrated*) *92*
Mémorial du Premier Siége (Larchey) *176–7*
Metternich, Prince Wenzel von 45
Michelin 79, 221
Middle Ages 6
Milk Tray Man 33
Minerva Café (Minerva Club) 7, *95*
Ministry of Food 49, *150*, 151, 155
Minney, R. J. *158*
Mitterand, François 161, 207, *218*, 219
Modern Cookery for Private Families (Acton) *132*, 133
The Modern Housewife (Soyer) 135
Modernism 195
molecular gastronomy 221
Monroe, Marilyn 105
Montgomery, H. Greville *190*
Moonraker 205
Moore, Thomas Sturge *196*, 197
Morelli, Giuseppe 61
Mountbatten, Louis (Lord Mountbatten) *102*, 103
A Moveable Feast (Hemingway) 199
Mugaritz 221
multi-sensory food *76*, 79

Nansen, Dr Fridtjof *13*
Napoleon III 175, 193
NASA 11
Nast, Thomas *208*
The National Health Service (HMSO) 124
Native Americans *188*, 189
neurogastronomy 63, *76*, 77
'A New Birth of Freedom' speech (Lincoln) 113
New York Public Library 66
NHS 81
    hospital food 115, 125
Nicholas II, Tsar 12, *162*, 163, *178*, 179, *180–1*, 213

Nissin *56*
Nixon, Richard 12, 105, 207, *216*, 217
Nobel, Alfred 89
Nobel, Ludvig 89
Nobel Prize dinners 81, 83, 89
Noma 221
nouvelle cuisine 221

Obama, Barack 83, *112*, 113, 173
Old Orchard Beach Restaurant 201
Osteria Francescana 221

Pacific Railway, US *29*
Pan Books *158*
Paris Siege (1870) 163, *174*, 175, *176–7*
Passy, Frédéric *88*, 89
Pâtisserie de la rue de la Paix 167
Patten, Marguerite 81, 131, *154*, 155
Perley, Benjamin 172
Perley's Reminiscences (Perley) 172
Picasso 11
Picasso, Olga (née Khokhlova) 195
Picasso, Pablo 185, *194*, 195
The Picture of Dorian Gray (Wilde) 193
pièces montées 167
Pier Casino and the Palace 201
Pitman Vegetarian Hotel, Birmingham 77
Plarr, Victor *196*, 197
popcorn *36*, 37
Pot Noodle 57
Potato Pete *130*
Pound, Ezra *196*, 197
Presley, Elvis ('The King') 6, 12, 161, 163, *182*, 183
Presley, Priscilla (née Beaulieu) 6, 161, 163, *182*
Prohibition 47, 115, 121
Prudhomme, Sully *88*, 89
Puck 50–1
Pullman Company *26*, 27

Queen Mary, RMS ('Ship of Woods') *74*, 75, *75*
Queen Victoria's Diamond Jubilee Luncheon 81, 83, *84*, 85, *85*, *86*, 87

R. Banks *16*
Ranhofer, Charles *18*, 19, 64, 65, *67*
Rasputin, Grigori 207, *212*, 213
Rayburn, Sam *110*
ready meals 54, 55, 147
ready-to-serve food 147
Red Cross 89
    canteen food (US) 115, *116*, 117, *118–19*
    First World War canteen (Britain) 81
Red's Giant Hamburg *53*
Redzepi, René 221
Regency dinner (1804) 163, *166*, 167
The Representation of the People Act (1918) 95
'The Revolt of Islam' (Shelley) 159
The Ritz 11, 15, 63, *68*, 69, 79
Ritz, Caesar 69
roadside restaurants 17, *40*, 41
Roca, Joan 221
Romanov family 12, *162*, 163, *178*, 179, *180–1*, 213
Röntgen, Wilhelm Conrad *88*, 89
Roosevelt, Franklin D. ('FDR') 11, 83, *96*, 97

Roosevelt, Theodore 27
Rothko, Mark 109
Route 66 53
Routledge *134*
Roux, Michel 129
Rowntree's Black Magic 33
Royal Albert Hall 185, *188*, 189
Royal College of Music (RCM) 189
Royal Pavilion, Brighton 167, *168–9*
Royal Swedish Academy of Music 89
Russian Revivalist movement 179

Sacher, Eduard 45
Sacher, Franz, Jr 45
Sacher, Franz, Sr 45
Salinger, J. D. 185, *202*, 203
Sampson Low, Son, and Marston 140
sandwiches, packaged pre-made 57, *58*, 59
Saturday Evening Post 48
Saturday-night fast food 17, 39
Saturday Supper 203
Savage Club 13, *184*, 185, *188*, 189, *190–1*
Savage, Richard 189
Savoy 69, 99
A Scandal in Bohemia (Conan Doyle) 193
school dinners 11, 115, *122*, 123
Scotland Yard 205
Scott's of Mayfair *204*, 205
Second World War 35, 49, 75, 99, 125, *130*, 155, 205, 219
self-service 77
service à la Russe 17, *18*, 19, *20–1*
Shaw, George Bernard 131, *158*, 159
Shelley, Percy 159
Sherlock Holmes *192*, 193
Sherman, Gen. William Tecumseh 209
Shilling Cookery for the People (Soyer) *134*, 135
Ship of Woods, see Queen Mary, RMS
The Sign of Four (Conan Doyle) 193
Simpson, Wallace 193
Sinatra, Frank 105, 109
Smith, Delia 133
Sound of the Sea 79

Southern Pacific Lines *107*
Southern Railway Company 8
Soyer, Alexis 135
Soyer's Charitable Cookery (Soyer) 135
Soyer's Shilling Cookery for the People (Soyer) *134*, 135
space food 115, 127
Spang, Rebecca L. 9
Sparkman, John *108*, *110*
Stalin, Joseph 11, 83, *96*, 97, 105
Steinbeck, John 109
Stoddart, J. M. 193
The Strand Magazine 192
strawberries and cream 15, 17, 31
Suffragettes' Victory Dinner (1918) 83, *94*, 95
Surrealism 185
Swanson & Sons *54*, 55

Taj Palace Hotel *102*, 103
takeaway food 17, *38*
Talleyrand-Périgord, Charles Maurice de 167
Tatler 77
Taylor, Elizabeth 75, 105
Tehran Conference (1943) 83, *96*, 97
Thomas, Dylan 189
Thomas, Jerry 47
Throne and Country 30
Titanic, RMS *206*, 207, *210*, 211
Toronto Star Weekly 199
'Tour of the President Through the Northwest' (Pullman) *26*
Tower Café Restaurant, Blackpool *72*, 73
Treasure Trove in Tins *153*
trenches food 81, 83, *90*, 91
TV dinners *54*, 55, 57, 147
Twain, Mark 189, 193

UN Peace Dinner (1946) 83, *98*, 99, *100–1*
'The Union Christmas Dinner' (Nast) *208*
United Nations (UN) 99

The Valley of Fear (Conan Doyle) 192
Van Buren, Martin 173

van 't Hoff, Jacobus H. *88*, 89
Vasnetsov, Viktor 179
vegetarian restaurants/food 7, 63, 76, 77, 131, *158*, 159
Vegetarian Society 77
Victoria, Queen 81, 83, *84*
Vogler, Pen 2
Vogue 195
The Vote 95
The Voyage of the Beagle (Darwin) 170

Wagner, Mrs 201
Waldorf-Astoria 46, 47, *70*, 71
Waldorf Salad 71
Walloon Lake, Michigan 198
Wall's 61
Walsh, J. H. *20*
The War Illustrated 92
wartime food 81, 115, 116, 117, *118–19*, 131, 135, *150*, 151, *152–3*, 155
Watergate scandal 217
wedding breakfast *182*, 183
Wenberg, Ben 64
West Sussex Gazette 35
The West Wing 173
White House 12, 83, *109*, 113, 161, 207, *216*, 217
White Star Line 206
Wilde, Oscar 161, 185, 193
Wimbledon 15, 30, 31
Winter Palace, St Petersburg 179
'Wise Eating in Wartime' (Ministry of Food) 150
Women's Freedom League (WFL) *94*, 95
Women's Institute (WI) 17, *34*, 35
Wood, Lawson *188*
World's Best Restaurant 79

Ye Old Cheshire Cheese 197
Yeats, W. B. *196*, 197
yuletide feasts/food, see Christmas
Yusupov, Felix 213

zakuski 213

The last guest.